James A. Fink

I AM
ENOUGH

A Gay Guy's Truths

I dedicate this book to

all of the closeted bigots & haters,

I see your judgements.

Give me a moment. It's all I ask of you!

And...

for all who feel excluded in life, may you find

HOME!

PROLOGUE

. . . .

Flat on my back, out of breath, sweat rolling down my face, the room hot and humid with the smell of sex lingering in the air. As I look around, it's as if everything was just flipped upside down in a police raid. The sheets are spread half on the bed, with the remaining draping over to the floor, as if torn apart in a rage of anger. As I lay amongst the sheets of madness, trying to catch my breath, I begin to comprehend what just happened. As my eyes open, staring down at me is a gorgeous tawny brown Latino man in his mid to late twenties. He is approximately six foot one, and his build is slender, with a slightly under-toned stomach. His body hair is perfectly groomed and runs up from his thick, uncircumcised penis, straight to his chest. His hair is short, chestnut brown and precisely groomed, with fresh, crisp edges. Those eyes! Oh, those eyes, caramel brown with flexes of honey mustard yellow. They are so mesmerizing that I become lost in thought, looking into them as if they were stars in the clear night skies. Just like

1

Dante himself, they're so soft and gentle. His smile is so cheeky that when he grins, his dimples become deep, and are plainly visible through his 5 o'clock shadow. When Dante smiles, you can see a perfect gap in his top front teeth.

Everything about him causes me to become overwhelmed, yet content, all at the same time. Dante stares at me like I'm the only thing in the world that matters to him. It feels like love is looking directly into my eyes, and I'm one of the luckiest men alive. As he stares at me, his body is still glistening in a perfect sheen of salty sweat. As it rolls down his physique, he has the most erotic aroma of sex lingering on him. The silence is so present in the room that the only sound you can hear is our heavy breathing. All I can do is gaze at this man's beautiful features. The slight dip in his chin, the space between his front teeth, and not to mention those dimples, all seem to have me in a complete state of infatuation.

At this moment, all I want to do is take his brawny long-haired arms and wrap them around me in the hope that Dante never lets me go. All I've ever wanted is to have a feeling of comfort and security from a man who loves me for who I am. Being my true self, living my authentic life, with no more lies, no more secrets, and no more feelings of deception is what I need, and Dante does this for me. All I want is what I just had, a hawt steamy "fuck" session with the most amazing man who won't make me feel insecure afterward.

These moments - of having our hot glistening bodies, in their natural form, with no over-grooming, no excessive muscle, our natural musk filling the air, and us clawing at each other like animals tearing each other's clothes off - have my heart racing. As I lie face down on the bed, Dante spreads my pasty, warm butt cheeks like a steamy hotdog bun, and begins eating me so hard and fierce that his tongue feels like a sex toy penetrating my hole. With that, I begin to moan so loud that, even with my face buried in the pillow, I am sure that neighbors the next block down can still hear my muffled moans of ultimate pleasure. As fast as he begins working on the back door, he flips me over and begins swallowing my throbbing cock. Six inches is as deep as he can possibly go before gagging on the girth and bringing tears to his eyes.

His motions and actions are hot and heated, yet so passionate at the same time. Dante slowly licks his way from my hardened, wet, and pulsating cock, right up to my lips. My musk is so present as he gently kisses my lips and lightly begins licking them, like soft-serve ice cream running down the cone. Dante teases me with light nibbles on my lips, and in the next instant, he begins sucking on my tongue like he is savoring a piece of delicious milk chocolate. So erotic, and so turned on, yet Dante won't let me reciprocate any of what he is doing to me. Still, with my tongue in his mouth, he begins to slide his hand down over my pudgy and sparsely hair-covered stomach. He passes right over my extremely engorged cock and down to my welcoming anus.

Already sweaty, Dante takes his left index finger and enters me; I gasp with both shock and pleasure as he slowly thrusts it in and out of me. Within moments he turns me over on my stomach and quickly begins rubbing personal lubricant all over my waiting and willing hole. Just moments after, I feel his rock-hard seven-inch uncircumcised cock burrowing deep inside my tunnel of darkness. Now he is looking for some reciprocation and my full participation. He wastes no time entering all the way in and I now feel his big hairy ball sack against mine. I begin to push back towards him, rocking my "cushion for the pushing" back and forth.

Within moments he is thrusting hard and deep. The sound of his nuts slapping against mine is so arousing that pre-cum is running out of my cock all over the gray bed sheets. The sound of his grunting and moaning is such a turn-on; it is feeding all my sexual senses at once. My only wish at that moment is for it to last forever. His thrusting continues until I can hear him beginning to moan louder and louder, declaring that he is about to cum. In that instant, I demand that he blow his warm salty seed deep within me. With just those words, he grabs my hips so hard I can feel his fingernails digging into me. My ass is now pulled tight to his body; he is entirely inside of me and yelling, "Fuck, I'm cumming!" In that second, I feel the warm pulse and release of his seed so deep inside of me, it is as if I can taste his thick load in my mouth. He falls on top of me with exhaustion, sweaty, sticky, dirty and I love every minute of it.

My eyes open wide, my heart racing, perspiration running down my face and the sheets soaked from night sweats. What just happened? Just a dream, the dream of what I thought being an out gay man could be like. These dreams are so vivid, it is as if I can smell the sweet scent of sex lingering in the air of my bedroom. These are recurring dreams at night and daydreams during the day, as I often catch myself gazing out lost in this world. Fuck! This was how I thought it could be when I came out as my true self. This couldn't have been any further from the truth.

FINDING THE LIGHT

· ·

CHAPTER 1

"Everyone gets second chances, but not everyone takes them"

S itting alone, staring, my eyes welling with sadness and fear of what had been building up inside me for many years. As the tears began to fall slowly down my plump pale face, I could feel the warm salty stream running down through my ginger scruff. It's as if the stream of tears was an emotional game of Plinko on, "The Price is Right," except my tears were the Plinko chips, and there was no prize to be won, even with my tears perfectly running down my neck and to my chest, landing right between my "man boobs." Suddenly, there was the loud honk of a horn from the seemingly impatient driver of the vehicle behind me, startling me from my deepened thoughts of fear. When I came to, I saw that the red stoplight had now turned green. I pressed on the gas pedal to proceed en-route to work, where I was a cleaner for a local casino. The drive had become a familiar routine almost every day of the year 2010.

It's as if my daily life was on repeat. Hopelessness and being trapped were feelings that never seemed to stop haunting me. For many years they just continued to grow in their intensity. All these emotions rendered me unable to drive to my mundane job without crying. Crying always seemed to come from my thoughts of what it would be like to love life fully; living the way I could only dream would make me truly happy - feeling that I needed to be freed from the locked emotional chest deep down within me. The fear of taking a chance and changing the whole dynamic of my family was so much to bear. It felt like I was beginning to wither away inside. The tears falling were never typical tears of sadness; they were streams of massive emotional pain, and they fell everyday. They caused me moments of pulling over to the side of the road, while passersby would just look over at me and stare. The image, from their point of view, was that of a full-grown, six-foot-tall, three hundred-fourteen pound, caucasian, ginger man; sitting in his burgundy rusted-out mini-van at the shoulder of the road, with heavy tears rolling from his red and puffy eyes.

This, my daily routine, was now becoming so intense, that not only would my emotional breakdowns happen on my way to work, but would resume on the drive home. I would dry my face just in time to return to the reality of my wife Connie and our four young children. In my day-to-day life, I already felt like a failure as a father; living penny to penny, so poor it was a struggle even to feed my family. Now, on top of it all, I had become so miserable with myself and with life, the only thing I could do was eat away my feelings to the point of morbid obesity: so obese that, even lying on my back to sleep generally caused me to lose my breath. Most of my evenings and nights included flopping on the bed, eating myself sick, and watching old sitcom reruns of shows I could relate to. Secluding myself from Connie and the children was an attempt to evade even further pain, seeing them smile reminded me that everything could soon change. Every day I wondered if not waking up would be better than the pain I would soon cause my family.

My continual overeating was the pathway to a slow and natural death, and seemed the best option for me at the time. It gave me a sense of comfort, knowing that, in a way, I would still be there for my children, at least for now. My income was the primary support for my family, so thoughts of "What would happen if?" Often crossed my mind. If I committed suicide, would my children grow up wondering if it was something they did wrong? Would they wonder why their father no longer wanted to be alive and be a family with them and mom? Would suicide due to personal unhappiness be worth the lifetime of pain for my children? The answers were always the same, and I had to push on. The love for my children was great, and it was my obligation and responsibility to take care of them no matter what. It's "I love you to the moon and back," not "I love you to my grave, and that is that." Even now, there are still very few things I would not do for my children. I refused to be a stereotypical "deadbeat" parent, knowing all too well the pain it causes. Having lived with my father's absence for the majority of my life, I knew the pain. So for me, being home at the end of the day was a necessity.

Returning home to a family I loved dearly, all while feeling miserable, and wondering what I could do to make us feel whole, complete, and loved, was a heavy burden. Seeing my children's faces and hearing them yell "Dad!" every day when I would come in the door was a euphoric feeling. Sometimes it was not possible to match their enthusiasm, because my undiagnosed, untreated depression was masking most of my emotions. There was a constant gnawing feeling buried deep inside, knowing that I could hurt my family through revealing my sexuality. I will always be extremely grateful to my ex-wife Connie for giving me my four children, regardless of our differences and my sexuality.

Knowing that I could not be who I longed to be for so many years tore me up inside. The degree of that pain caused not only tears but other health issues both mental and physical. I yearned to be a man, able to show genuine love for someone regardless of gender, and still be a dad. I wanted nothing more than to spend my years raising my kids, while living with a person that I was truly in love with.

My truth hurts so intensely, that even today, it brings tears to my eyes. Therefore, how could I expect my family to ever understand what had to be released from deep within me? Telling the truth to my wife was the first step that had to be taken, as not only was living this way not fair to me, it was not fair to her.

Once I built up the courage to tell Connie, I knew, from that moment on, my life would be forever changed. Not knowing how this would affect my children was one of the hardest things to think about and overcome. Waiting so long to express how I genuinely felt took so many years, due to my belief that you have to finish what you start in life. However, I began my family when I was only fifteen years old, with someone who is thirteen years my senior. Being so young, I believed I knew it all, and I would prove to anyone and everyone who said I couldn't do it, that I could and would. My drive and determination were strong to prove I could succeed and show the disbelievers that I was not my father. Unlike him, I was very proud of my family and am still incredibly proud of my children.

Connie and I had many differences throughout our marriage: even so, I felt that I couldn't leave her. She was part of my life, and we created four spectacular children together. I did not employ deception or lies to be less than straightforward and open about my sexuality. The realization and understanding of who I was, wasn't discovered until later in life. My children were born before I understood that I was attracted to men, and this attraction was not just in a way that was like, "Wow! That's a handsome man." It was more like, "Holy Shit! Come on over here, you sexy beast." When these moments started, so did the understanding that I was a gay man, feeling as if I were a hormone-filled teenager, catcalling men walking down the street.

Although I had a home, steering from my family life was not an option, nor was allowing my hormones to take dominance over me. One of the things I'm personally proud of through my whole journey, is that I can go to my grave with the knowledge that I was never unfaithful in any way to my wife, or any other partner I've had. People pass the blame on to me, saying I was deceitful to my wife, and to that, I say, no! No matter what is or was said, I was never that. I was a confused, hormonal, fourteen-year-old boy when I started having sex with my twenty-seven-year-old girlfriend, who later became my wife. At that age, I didn't know who I was. Hell, I hadn't even finished puberty, let alone discovered I was gay. Looking back on it, I was like any teenage boy, in "lust" with what societal pressures make you believe you need to be, and that for me was, "straight."

When the time came, and there was a vagina in front of me, as a horny teenager, I went with it. Ten months from the first time Connie and I had sex, our first child was conceived; I was just fifteen years old at the time. In the autumn of 1998, at the age of sixteen, my first child, a daughter, came into this world. Proud, amazed, overwhelmed and scared are the only emotions that describe how I felt when she was born. Knowing that I was responsible for this fantastic, tiny human, was mind-blowing.

Most of what I knew in life was quickly changing. I was no longer attending high school, nor did I get to graduate with my friends. My new priority was finding a job close to our one-bedroom home, which was an old summer cottage converted into a year-round house. Our home was no more than 500 square feet, and a twenty-minute walk to the town's only grocery store. We had no vehicle, and neither of us had a driver's license or the money to afford a car, or the insurance on one. Even with me working, there was never enough money to pay the bills, buy food, clothing or pay our rent on time.

Due to these money issues, we had to move in the middle of 1999, and we ended up in a place even more secluded than our previous home. There was not a store within walking distance for buying groceries or odds and ends. That same year, when I was seventeen years old, we found out that we were expecting our second child. Only one month after my eighteenth birthday in the spring of 2000, my second daughter came into the world. Now a father to two beautiful girls, the stress grew even more extreme. Ten months and another house later, at the beginning of 2001, we were expecting baby number three. My third and youngest daughter was born in the fall of the same year, when, at nineteen years of age, I was barely old enough to legally purchase tobacco and alcohol in Canada. So at a time when my former schoolmates were at the bars buying and drinking alcohol, I was already a father of three wonderful daughters. Only weeks after my third daughter was born, we had to move again, as the sheriff had evicted us. In 2002, we discovered we were expecting our fourth and final child. We welcomed our son in the spring of 2003, just two days before my twenty-first birthday; now, with four children under the age of 5, our family was complete.

Connie and I talked about having a fifth baby, but with the birth of each child, things became more challenging. I took it upon myself to book a vasectomy without telling Connie. My baby-making days ended on Friday, June 13, 2003. As I stared up at one doctor and two very young medical students while they performed my procedure, I felt awkward to say the least. After a vasectomy, you're not supposed to lift more than ten pounds for the first few days, but we once again had to move, and I had to lift ninety percent of the furniture on my own. After this, my Johnson was so black and blue from the broken blood vessels and torn stitches. I don't recommend not following doctors' orders.

Looking back, I wonder how I managed to raise four children born within six years of each other. We lived in more than ten homes, and stayed with friends at least twice between 1998-2010, and from 2011 to the present, we have lived in an additional eight homes, and stayed with friends and family twice. So, perhaps life became so busy during the years of 1998-2010. When my children were being conceived, born, and raised, that I couldn't focus on myself and my sexual feelings towards men. No matter how horny and turned on I was by men, nothing would cause me to be unfaithful to my family. Knowing that the future would be uncertain if I were to come out scared me, as I loved my kids and didn't want to hurt their little souls in any way. My mind was constantly flooded with memories of times of happiness. Now, I had to figure out how to unlock the truth for all to see, with as little disruption to my children as possible.

These thoughts caused much depression that I hid; maybe not well, but I did try to hide it. There was no turning back once I opened my mouth about my sexuality; once out there, it could no longer be erased or hidden. Telling my kids the truth wasn't the most challenging part of coming out. It would be telling them that, due to dad's sexuality, Mom and Dad are getting divorced. Crushing my children's tiny spirits, because mom and dad would no longer be together, was killing me inside. I tried my best: I was such a young parent, and my true sexuality was coming to light, along with the beginnings of acceptance. I tried for years to keep my family dynamic together, as I genuinely believed it was expected of me. It was like, "You made your bed. Now you have to lie in it." Having had an absent father most of my life, I didn't want to make the same mistakes that he had. No, my father is not gay, but he made mistakes. He was a largely absent parent, contributed little to the family dynamic, and never fostered a relationship with me.

In my early to mid-twenties, I thought that I was bisexual, and that made everything normal, because a bisexual male was still attracted to females. After a year of deceiving myself, it was becoming clear that I was not sexually attracted to women. When the reality kicked in that I was, in fact, gay, I decided to stay hidden, primarily because I didn't want to crush my family dynamic, even though I knew, at some point, change would be inevitable. I can't recall the exact date and time when I realized I was gay, but I know it was somewhere around 2009. My secret stayed just that - I did not want my children to grow up like the other children at school. Most of the kids they knew had parents that were divorced or no longer together. Of course, I guess I would be finally giving my kids something their friends had; divorced parents.

Jokes aside, I wanted my children to be proud of their family, knowing that mom and dad were together, and most of all, happy. The ideal was for my children to see, no matter how tough times got, that they had a complete family, who celebrated the holidays together with love. My feelings of responsibility to make sure that my kids were loved and all under one roof together was very strong. The most important part for me was to be sure my kids wouldn't have to be split up into separate homes, or flip-flop from one parent's home to the other on weekends. These thoughts kept me from having the drive to change my life, even though it would essentially make my children's lives better. Having a happy father would make them happy, too, right? Not knowing what would happen once I came out, I felt I should do as little as possible regarding my marriage with Connie. I had to plan how or when to make these massive life changes and put them into action. I still took care of my daily responsibilities, but I no longer went above and beyond, knowing Connie would soon have to step up. I always felt as if I was making mistakes as a father, and perhaps ruining my children's ideas of what a perfect family should be. We didn't have the money to buy them what other children had. This continuously added to the feeling that I was a failure. This was one of my biggest challenges to try and overcome, and now I was taking the chance of having them hate me forever!

Preparing for parenthood at fifteen, and becoming a father at sixteen, life became astronomically tough. I often became physically ill, crouching down on the bathroom floor, poised over the toilet, to throw up. The anxiety was like having a hangover all day, every day. At the time I thought these feelings were due to the stress caused by our finances. In reality, it was a combination of financial worries and the unhappiness I felt deep within me. Increasing sadness and depression was magnified by daily phone calls from creditors, adding fear to my whirlwind of thoughts. I had to keep a roof over my kid's heads with the power on, while dealing with the knowledge of who I indeed was on the inside. It all felt like a hurricane waiting to happen without a moment's notice.

My thoughts on those daily drives to work were always: how would my children feel, knowing they had no place to live, no electricity, no heat, and almost no food in the cupboards? How could I explain that Dad doesn't love Mom any longer, at least not in the same way they once knew? How could I tell them their dad is attracted to men, and wants to be with a man instead of a woman? Children are resilient, even when so very young, but still I didn't know how they would react. All I did know was that I felt like I was dying inside. Some days all I wanted to do was die; I had many suicidal thoughts when I was married. I was miserable: my true sexuality was emerging and becoming more pronounced. The pain deep down within me was so much to take. I felt I wasn't enough. I couldn't keep us from being evicted from our home or having our utilities turned off, and I felt that this was always my fault. No matter what age I was, sixteen to twenty-six, it always felt that way.

For the longest time, I never recognized the issues within our marital relationship, as I thought it was my job, no matter what age, to take care of my family. Maybe this came from not having a father around when I was growing up to lead the way and show me what a positive and healthy relationship was. I'm not pointing fingers at my father for my dysfunctional relationship. I know that, for many reasons, some people don't have a father figure in their life while growing up, yet have incredibly healthy relationships as adults. Nor do I blame my mother for my choices when growing up. Even though I was young and naive, I accept responsibility for my actions. The only thing that kept me from taking my life was knowing that my children would be left not knowing why, why did their father choose to take his life and leave them behind? In the back of my mind, I knew that if I left this world there would be a good chance my children would not be adequately taken care of. This isn't saying that I was the best father, or that they were always taken care of with high standards, but I would always make sure they would have at least the basics growing up. From my experiences, I just knew that they would struggle to have any positive life with their mother if I wasn't there.

I've shed many tears, hidden behind closed doors, wondering, How? When? Who would be affected by my coming out? That is, if I could bring myself to do so. My whole life growing up, I always said to myself, no matter how I felt inside, I would never come out as gay. I was always fighting my fear of being gay: the world was too cruel to let me be out and happy. Many people could do things to me to try and take that happiness away or crush it. The actions of others could also affect my children, and I would be devastated if that happened. Daydreaming about how life could be if I wasn't stuck in the closet, and instead, living in an ideal world, was all I could ever do. I never thought that one day I would be brave enough to make my dreams a reality; well, to a certain point anyway. It may not have been the ideal reality, but at least it was the reality of not having those prolonged feelings trapped inside me. I could show everybody the man I truly was meant to be, and raise my children to be strong, independent people.

My children were accepting and loving, not only to me, but to everybody else involved. My children's strength was incredible. Seeing how, even at such young ages, they had the power and understanding to know everything would be okay. From the sidelines, I would watch and listen to them; it was like they had their own support team between the four of them. They supported each other as changes were happening in the home. Connie and I were always there to answer any questions they had, and we did our best to make them feel loved and secure. When I look back on how they dealt with things, I don't think they know how much support they were to each other. Even at their ages now, I don't know if they see that.

I think my extended family took it harder than my children did. This was most likely because they expected my children would go through a hard time. Their perception was that my morals would change along with my sexuality, causing my kids to suffer. Many of the outsiders in my family thought that I would become a "Slut" or a "Whore" believing that I would be sleeping with anyone that had a hard penis and potentially ending up with HIV and other STIs, just because I was gay. So many people have narrow views and believe that, just because you're gay, you will be promiscuous, and you will end up ill or hurt. Yes, this can be the reality for some gay people, just as it can be for someone of any sexuality. Their fears and concerns were valid: these health issues have always been a large part of the gay community. But their worries also came from a lack of knowledge.

In their eyes, all they were trying to do was help. This was as helpful as two virgins trying to teach each other the importance of foreplay. My family was caring, but they weren't sensitive about how to handle it. They were using the stereotypes of what they thought being gay was all about. Just because a person is gay, it doesn't mean they're handed a manual telling them what to do to be out and proud. I think my family believed there was such a book, and if not followed, there would be a list of consequences. The manual they must have been thinking about was that mythical book, called the Bible. All I wanted was people to accept me for me, especially my family and friends.

So I was guilty. Guilty of wanting more, and feeling I needed more to be happy. I knew something had to change, and that change had to begin with me. It would be the start of me living a better life, not only for my health, but for my children, who were between the ages of seven and twelve at the time. My start would be a weight loss journey that began in December 2010; a journey I never thought I would have the strength to accomplish. I figured this would just be another failure, causing another push to hide even further. Yet, to my surprise, not only would I succeed, but this is where I began to see the light.

My determination for permanent change was thriving. By the end of 2010, I was down approximately thirty pounds by diet only, and my drive started to increase even further when I saw what I could accomplish, especially because this was something that most people said I couldn't do. During the first month of changes, I began to think a lot about complete happiness, but I knew that I couldn't rock the house during the holiday season. At the start of January 2011, I decided to ramp up my weight loss by adding daily walks. These walks were intensive for my mind as well as my body: walking alone has always tended to help clear my head and organize my thoughts. What can I say? I walked a lot, almost every day of the week, and between ten to twenty-five kilometers a day. After only one week into the new year, I could start to feel a new me. During this time, I knew that neither my wife nor I was happy, and on Sunday, January 9, 2011, it happened.

On Saturday, January 8, the kids had settled into bed, and my wife and I were sitting in the living room of our home. Neither of us was happy, and we were showing signs of being very agitated with one another. Our conversation started with me asking her what was on her mind, in hopes that I could help with whatever it was. I was also hoping deep down that she would ask me the same question for a change, as that was rare. We went through things that were bothering Connie, and ideas on how to correct some of them. Our conversation went on for hours, and it was now past midnight. My wife, through her tears, looked at me and mumbled a few words that I did not hear clearly, so I asked her if she could repeat what she said. She asked me if I was okay or if something was bothering me, as I seemed off. My heart was racing so fast I would have sworn I was having a heart attack. She looked at me and said,"What is it?", with panic in her voice. I struggled to gather myself to speak, and this caused her to start throwing ideas out to see if that would help me spit out whatever I had to say. I just remember saying,"No, no! Nothing like that, but what I have to say will change our lives forever." She said,"Okay! What is it?"

One last deep breath from me, and I said it. I looked at her and said those three words, "I am gay." When I said it, it was the first time saying it aloud, as I had never even said the words to myself in the mirror. Hearing myself say,"I am gay," out loud was like hearing it echoing in an empty stadium, in slow motion, with the anticipation of at least one person way in the back standing up and saying something. Thoughts of "Holy Shit! I finally said it!" flooded my head. I can't say that I felt a weight off my shoulders at that time, knowing that I would have to break my kid's hearts with the news of mom and dad separating. It was out, and I felt as though I couldn't even breathe.

After that moment, I don't remember much except the discussions about the kids, their school, living arrangements, and so on. We decided that I would live in the home with her and the kids until I found a suitable place to live that was large enough for the children. We also agreed on 50/50 custody for the kids; one week with Connie and the off week with me. We also decided that we would tell the kids about our separation together, but I would explain in more detail on a one-on-one basis with each of them.

So, after a very short night's rest, we decided to speak to the kids. It was the last day of the Christmas break from school, so it seemed like it would be best to break the news and get it done so the kids could start to process everything in their own way. As expected, they cried a lot, as did we. Knowing I was living in the home and sleeping in the same bed as mom seemed to help some. I think this gave them temporary relief, thinking we would stay together, after all. For approximately ten weeks we lived like this, until I secured a large, three-bedroom upper floor apartment in a duplex. In March of 2011, I moved out with just a few boxes in hand, my clothes, and a TV. Slowly, I gathered used items to start over with, as I would have my children with me every other week. It certainly wasn't perfect, but I made do, and this new chapter of my life was about to begin. Tears of both sadness and happiness flooded my face the first few days after moving out, especially when I stood in my apartment and looked around, knowing that I was now able to start to live the way I had only dreamt of before.

Not having my children with me every day was a significant adjustment, and extremely hard in the start, as silence in the house was something I had not been used to for thirteen years. Here I was, standing in a pretty empty apartment, in extreme silence, with just my thoughts. It took me well over a month to adjust to the new living arrangements; going from nothing and lonely, to crazy and on top of one another when the kids were there. We may have been on top of each other, but I felt the most at home when they were there. Now, to figure out how to be a single dad 50% of the month, manage work and still try to figure out life all over again. It wasn't until weeks after I moved into the new place that I built up enough courage to allow myself to start meeting people for coffee that I had met online. I had been out since January: now it was April, and I had still not kissed or touched a man in any sexual way, just as I never did in the thirteen years I was with Connie. I still couldn't allow myself. I had many hesitations due to guilt and fear of not knowing what it would be like. Guilt was a really large part of it, still feeling I owed faithfulness to Connie because she hadn't moved on with her life - I blamed myself for that.

Connie and I stayed friends and tried to support each other from the start. This was a tricky situation, but we again made it work. Everyone in life gets a second chance, but not everyone takes it. I was given a whole new start, and I wasn't going to let it pass me by after all these years. Connie, on the other hand, let it pass her by often, and it was sad to watch. We had many talks about it in the first few years; about her taking chances and moving forward. Connie would often mention how it would never be the same, and she didn't know if she could trust again. After many months of trying to help Connie, I had to stop in order to move forward with the life I'd been waiting on. This life I had been longing for was finally a reality, yet here I was, still not living it to the fullest because I was being guilted by my ex, who refused to seek outside help. I was still that child who had married a grown adult, trying to be the person who always took care of Connie. Her dependency on me had to stop, but the guilt of what I did to my family allowed this dependency to carry on for a few years.

My love for Connie was there, but was it genuine love for her? Or was it love for the connections we had over the years with the kids, and the complacency of life together for thirteen years? It was a sweet and sour situation: there was love for Connie, yet there was also so much anger, and some hate. No matter what, I wouldn't be who I am today without her. Whether it had a negative or positive impact on my life, truth be told, it has molded me into the man I am today.

GOING IN BLIND

··

CHAPTER 2

"No experience is ever wasted,
everything has meaning"
~Oprah Winfrey

Before I came out as a gay male, I never thoroughly thought about the relationship aspects. Primarily it was the thought of having sex with a man, since that was something that I had never done, or even tried before. I knew how to be in a relationship, or at least I thought I did - my relationship with my ex-wife, Connie, wasn't very healthy. When I was coming out, I never really gave the relationship part of it a second thought. I was a dating virgin; the idea never crossed my mind, as I hadn't been on a date before, unless I was to count the one I had when I was eleven. When I was fourteen, I met Connie, and I was with her exclusively, right up until my coming out at the age of twenty-eight. There were a few crushes before that, but I wouldn't consider them relationships, especially since they werc mostly before I was even a teenager. There were no lessons on healthy communication or learning how to date in those twenty-eight years, let alone how to date another guy. So, sex was what I thought about 80% of the time.

Unconsciously, I was looking for a genuine connection with someone, but to make that happen, I figured there had to be sex, or I would lose the potential suitor. After more than a decade, it's easy to see that sex is nothing but just that. If a guy wants sexual gratification, he only needs to pull out his cock and send a picture on a hookup app, and he could have it within the hour. Just like a pizza, hot and ready! Unfortunately, there is no app designed to give you a meaningful connection with someone. It doesn't matter what any man or app says they have to offer. So, off I went, never having had sex, let alone a relationship with a man. I was going in blind!

Finally, this is it, and it's going to happen just like all the times I dreamt about it. My hormones were raging, and caused me to be so pent up and, well, horny. Oh my! This is it! This is how my first sexual experience with a man was going to go, and I could already envision it.

My heart is racing, and my body begins to sweat. The aroma of his musk is already driving me wild, thus making me want his body, and the large throbbing uncut cock attached to him. His cock is an aphrodisiac. My lips are running up and down his sweaty body. The smell of the pheromones coming up off of his playground makes me go mad with horniness. As I stare down, all I can see are his veins, plump and full of blood, inside his massive, erect cock. I want it! I want that cock down my throat. I want to taste that salty cum that is running out from the head of his joystick. I want it, and want it now! He throws me down on my bed, straddling my chest and pinning down my arms, all while forcing his hard enormous shaft down my throat; forcing me to taste his delicious seed.

As he thrusts his cock in and out of my wet warm mouth, I spit my warm saliva, now mixed with his cum, onto my fingers, and insert it in his tight, firm ass. Moaning with excitement, he thrusts into my mouth harder. My eyes are now watering, and my free hand begins spanking his ass. He stops, pulls it out of my mouth, flips me over, pulling my still-clothed ass up to his waist and ripping my jeans and underwear down to my knees, spreading my ginger peach ass-cheeks, his tongue warm and strong as he starts sliding it in and out of my hole without missing a beat. Just as fast as this starts, he removes his tongue, replacing it with the head of his one-eyed snake. The pressure of his warm wet pre-cum-soaked head pushes deep into my hole; it hurts. I begin moaning both with pleasure and discomfort.

It's so big, I swear I can feel it inside my stomach. The walls of my dark tunnel feel as though they are Kim K's black leggings being pulled up over her big ass. He grunts, grabbing my hips, pulling my ass in tight to him - so tight I can feel his picture-perfect dark curly pubic hair rubbing *against my ass-cheeks. Along with the pubes is the feel of his sexy treasure trail of hair, going up to his navel and touching the round humps of my ass. As I moan, I whisper, "Harder!" He replies with "Harder, eh?" With a slap on my bare sweaty ass, he begins slamming his sword deep inside me, going in and out of me like a piston, and with each second, his moans become increasingly louder. Within minutes he begins moaning the words, "Oh fuck! Oh, fuck! I'm cumming!" At that moment, for the first time, I feel a hard penis throbbing inside me with a sensual squirting sensation deep within. It's as if I am losing my virginity all over again.*

He slumps over me, his cock still inside my hole, and kisses my back, as his hand reaches underneath me, grabbing my cock. My cock is engorged, and so wet with pre-cum, you would think I had already released multiple loads all over the ruby-red silk sheets. He grabs hold of my cock, and uses my warmed pre-cum as lube while stroking my cock so fast and hard, I can hardly contain myself. It feels as though, as I release this load, my eyes will roll to the back of my head, and I will begin to see stars. I exclaim that I'm going to blow my load, so he stops, flipping me over, and shoving my cock straight down his throat without missing a beat. Within seconds I erupt, spewing semen into this gorgeous man's mouth - a load so big, I can see a teardrop of cum on the corner of his glistening cherry red lips. He pulls up, and my cock slips out of his mouth. He swallows and says to me, "Salty," jokingly, with a wink. We lie there,

not saying a word, the scent of sex permeating the room;
the smell I yearned for for more than a decade.

Naturally, this was far from how my first sexual experience as a gay man actually went. If my first time had been even a fraction of what I always dreamed or imagined, I would have been ecstatic. The fantasy of my first sexual experience, and the reality, were complete polar opposites. My first experience was one that I certainly hope never happens to anyone, except maybe a cheating ex. My first time with a man was with a younger guy named Kyle. He was approximately nine years younger than me. This man was so self-absorbed, it was hard to tell if he had an enormous ego, or if he was simply as inexperienced as me. While having sex, Kyle acted like he was the only person in the room.

We met on a dating app in March of 2011, and by April, I was ready to take the plunge and meet him in person. This was when I learned that, meeting in person to get to know each other and have coffee, just means meeting up to fuck. Being so against hookups, this was already a turn-off. When we got back to my apartment for coffee, I could tell he was eager to get down to it. I was not overly attracted to Kyle, but not being a superficial person, and willing to see if the cliche about personality is true, I thought, "Why not fuck and see how it goes?" We were only back at my place for maybe thirty minutes before he mentioned moving it to the bedroom, and my thoughts were to get my first time done and behind me. Let's say that I would rather still be a gay virgin than have that first experience.

Kyle and I made our way to my bedroom, with all the lights on. The insecurities about my body after losing all the weight preyed on my mind as we began to undress each other. My skin was not tight and firm, due to my loss of over one hundred pounds. Stereotypically, you need to have a fantastic body to fit sexually within the gay community - at least that was my perception after months of talking to other men online. Kyle didn't have a fit body, either. He was slender and fully shaved, which is far from a turn-on for me. Once undressed, I dropped down to my knees to work his cock; I was momentarily shocked by the size of his dick. His description was completely different from what was now right in front of me, and about to go into my mouth. His penis was circumcised, approximately four inches in length, with the circumference of an adult man's thumb. He also had Hypospadias, a condition in which the opening of the penis is on the underside rather than the tip. His was just under the tip. His small cock wouldn't have been an issue had he not lied to me about it online. Anyway, I began sucking his cock of deception and disappointment, and as I was doing so, I thought about how it would feel having him reciprocate with some light licks and sucking of my cock.

As we moved onto the bed, he moved down to my cock for what I expected to be the most fantastic blow job of my life. Wow! Wrong again. Kyle gave the saddest blow job, though I had very little to compare it to. He gave a half-ass twenty to thirty-second work up on my dick, and that was it. I was like, "Dude! It takes more than five licks to get to the center of this lollipop!" My frustrations grew even greater when he tried to sit down and put my cock inside of him. This was nerve-wracking and exciting simultaneously, followed almost immediately by disappointment, since he didn't want to continue. He said my cock was too large, and he would have to work up to it. Not knowing any better, I apologized, and stupidly began to suck his dick again. Within minutes he was blowing a minuscule load of cum in my mouth. Once Kyle was finished, that was it; he was off duty, and I either had to complete the job myself, or just let myself grow some blue-balls. So I left it.

Disappointment doesn't even begin to express my feelings that night. Was it nerves on both our parts, or was this how gay sex was supposed to be? Of course, I also thought it might just be Kyle, but regardless, the experience left me confused. After this first sexual liaison with a gay man, I began to feel shame and guilt building again. I felt I was cheating on Connie, and that I broke up my family for this meaningless non-fuck with a man whose penis was way smaller than his ego. Why did I do this? How could I do this? I felt ashamed. What was I doing?

So, I did what many do in life - I faked it. Kyle and I continued to hang out for a few weeks after our failed sexual union. Looking back, I must have loved torture, but I think I was hoping that some form of spectacular sex would come out of it if I kept trying. Kyle just ended up showing me how self-centered he really was. What happened in the bedroom was for him, and him alone. He would always "let me" suck his "cock," and he would never return the favor. In the few weeks that we were hanging out, he never once made me cum, and he didn't seem to care at all. Hanging out with him was my way of killing a bit of the loneliness, yet I was setting myself up for a mental mind fuck.

My weight loss journey was still an ongoing process. I was six-foot, two hundred pounds, and I felt terrific about how far I had come. It felt like I was flying high in the sky, and then the blue would suddenly turn to black. Unfortunately, the black was the rage I felt because of this self-centered little prick of a man-child I was "seeing." Kyle and I went out one night for drinks and dancing with his friends. Here I was, a father of four, feeling like I was chaperoning immature teenagers. As Kyle and I were about to hit the dance floor, he turned to me, patted my stomach, and said, "You need to suck in your stomach a bit!".
I surprised myself that night by not walloping Kyle to the point of needing transport to a hospital - a wallop so hard, he would end up back inside his mother's mouth. Hopefully, this time she would swallow the shallow little prick. After that night, I just made small talk with Kyle through text messages. He was moving to a place hours away, and I soon wouldn't have to speak to him anymore. After his move, you can bet I deleted and blocked him on every social media platform, and erased his number from my phone.

This was a life lesson for me on what to never accept from anyone. Someone was making me feel less about myself because of their own insecurities. He could only feel better by making me feel lower. I told myself that I would let hell freeze over before allowing that into my life again. It was unfortunate; I failed to learn from that, and continued to allow it, many times over again, for about the first nine years of being out. More recently, I have learned not to take shit from any man, no matter what, even if he does give a mind-blowing blow job. My blunt attitude may keep me from meeting someone who could be the love of my life, but I refuse to let anyone make me feel low about myself again. You must love me for me, or feel free to go fuck yourself! This, my newest motto, after allowing so many shallow, sneaky and slimy men into my life. My worth is more than a fast and shitty orgasm from some two-pump chump, when I can do the deed better on my own.

Mental anguish and exhaustion aren't worth a few minutes of emotionless, empty sex with someone who is just in it for themselves. So, good and vigorous masturbation is part of my self-care routine; at least this way, my satisfaction is guaranteed. Masturbating is user-friendly, and doesn't require a "Masturbation for Dummies," manual. There have been men in my life who like to hammer their "prize possession" inside of me. Once, my boyfriend and I were having hot and heavy make-up sex after an argument. During this, "I'm sorry," sex session, his raging, hard penis slipped out of me. Instead of gently putting it back in, he rammed it in with brute force. This caused my backdoor to tear; thus, a heavy bleed began, as if I were a woman in the thick of her menstrual cycle. I thought I was going to have to place a tampon up my asshole, and eat a tub of Ben and Jerry's ice cream. After this incident, it was a few weeks before the garage door welcomed any vehicles inside.

Karma came for my boyfriend a short while later. It was time to make things a bit spicy in the bedroom, so how better to do it, than with a sex swing? The swing hung from the ceiling of our bedroom, with him, strapped in and ready for the ride. Our foreplay had just begun, both of us naked, and him in the swing, when, in the blink of an eye, WHACK! Down came the swing, with the metal swivel bar smacking him directly on the head. He wasn't seriously injured, but sweet Karma did pay a visit to him that night.

Back then, I seemed to enter (or push myself) into relationships for all the wrong reasons. Jumping right in gave me a rush of love and contentment; false or not. Many times, I've entered into one with the hope of my yearslong fantasy of the picture-perfect union; raising children together, and living happily ever after, behind a white picket fence. This, unfortunately, never was the case, as there was so much "baggage" dragged in from both sides. It's hard to create a life together, free from stress and unnecessary arguments, when you have so much of your past sitting right next to you. Not one of my relationships has ended with me thinking that I was doing the wrong thing. Of course, any breakup hurts, and one can't help but wonder what could have been done differently, or what changes would have brought mutual happiness.

I often feel I failed myself for not looking at the larger picture, and for not taking note of all the red flags in my relationships. All too often, when starting over with someone new, I was guilty of "painting the red flags green." It seemed easier to ignore the warnings and hope for the best. Then later, I would beat myself up for not going with my initial gut feelings. If the person you're seeing is talking to other men behind your back, it's easier to blame yourself, thinking you must be doing something wrong. Otherwise, they wouldn't go elsewhere. Maybe, if you change something about yourself they wouldn't want to wander. All too often, I ignored the flags or painted them green, because I never felt I was "good enough," but if I tried, maybe I could be. Since coming out, I've only experienced the, "Honeymoon phase," of a relationship, once. All the other times flags were waving right in my face, but I just ignored them. Some of the ones too big to ignore included:

- Smashing dinner glasses in front of my family at holiday dinners

- Threatening to hit me if I left the house when they didn't want me too

- Throwing themselves down entire flights of stairs, only to later claim I had pushed them

- Portraying themselves as sexually inexperienced with men or women, later confessing they had slept with more than 120 people before the age of twenty

- Asking to take my last name within the first month of the relationship

- Finding messages to their friends, discussing "flaws" in my body

- Finding messages requesting inappropriate pictures from men. Even after some of the recipients of these messages made a point of stating, "Aren't you in a relationship?", they replied, "So?"

- Having to call 911 when they are found, overdosed, because they didn't get what they wanted

- Not being able to leave the room without them following you

- Receiving marriage proposals within the first 60 days

- Having sex was only about themselves

- Having no job and/or any desire for one

- Never living outside of their parents home, and they're over the age of thirty

- Still living with their ex for months or even longer after their split

- Being rude to my children and making them cry

- Discovering their best friend is their "Spank Bank Material"

- Always talking about their ex

Maybe these aren't red flags to some people, but they were (and are) to me. Knowing a partner's sexual history is important to me, especially if we have reached the point of considering unprotected sex. Now, in this case, we had been together for over six months. I knew something was wrong, due to the way my boyfriend was acting. When I found out, I was naturally upset. I had been put at risk for STIs and HIV. They hadn't even been tested, though they said they had. Had I contracted something serious, this would have altered my life, as well as the lives of my children. I am, after all, a single father. That, right there, was a life lesson for sure: never trust anyone unless you see things for yourself. As for someone throwing themselves down the stairs, I'm very thankful there were witnesses when it happened.

The significance of the other things, like having no job, living at home, or living with an ex, really depends upon the situation. Most of the time, though, it seems to stem from becoming content with having someone do everything for them. Finally, when it comes to the "best friend," pay attention to the red flags. Do not, by any means, ignore them! Many times, including in my case, I found out later that they had a sexual relationship with the "friend," and were trying to get back with them. (And yes, if they still talk about their ex, they're not over them, no matter what they tell you.)

You wouldn't think it would be so hard to find someone with similar goals in life, but it is. Many men "temporarily" have goals like yours, but they're only the same until you get together and fuck: then "BAM" they suddenly want significantly different things out of life. I'm almost forty years old, and I still sit and wonder: if I had done something differently in one of my relationships, would it have changed the outcome? Is there someone out there who is my close-to-perfect other half? That person - so compatible that we will end up in that white-picket-fence scenario I have longed for for eighteen years of my life. It's challenging to sit every night and wonder if something I did has caused me to sit, single, unable to hold together a healthy relationship. Lying alone in bed is hard some nights, when all you want is the warm touch of a man and the words, "Everything will be okay," whispered in your ear. Yet sometimes, you have to accept that the warmest thing to touch your body may be your own tears.

Are my expectations too high when it comes to men and relationships? Maybe! Do I deserve these expectations, high or not? Of course I do! I've lived too long in the closet to lower my expectations of the person I want to spend the rest of my life with. Many people along the way have said I should give all men a chance, no matter what, when they come my way. Well, doing that is what gets me into trouble in the first place. I give a chance to everyone, but now - first red flag, and that's it. Wasting my time, and causing undue stress, is not needed. I am not a game that someone can play and put away whenever they feel like it. It gets to a point where life becomes all about pleasing everyone but yourself. You need to put yourself first, or you will set yourself up for failure, as I did multiple times. Online dating is the quickest way to meet someone, but also, the fastest way to ruin any faith you may have in yourself. People are incredibly nasty behind the keyboard, and unless you have great confidence, they will strip you like a piranha of whatever self-esteem you may have. So many times, I have wished for an easier way to meet people than online dating.

These dating sites and apps for your phone are basically like the "Help Wanted ads" in the newspaper. They all request the same information: a picture, a small bio if you want to add one, and personal information about yourself (some tend to overshare). In reality they should have a subtitle like "Looking To Fuck!" with an address, proposed time of interaction, and a picture of a cock and ass. That's it! At least it is straight to the point, and you know what you are dealing with. There are so many "Time Wasters" out there, and all they want to do is play up the "perfect relationship" they want with you, and then one day you're ghosted, and they're never to be heard from again.

When someone writes about themselves on a dating site, you take their words to be true, if you want to pursue something with them: it's the chance you must be willing to take. The majority of what you read and hear from people in the dating world is probably bullshit. Nothing they say is comparable to who they are in real life; everyone puts their best foot forward, but nobody writes the shitty stuff about themselves. The shitty stuff is the hard stuff - the baggage - and you either accept it or move on. People want to fuck, so if lies will get them what they want, they won't ever speak the truth. If people were straightforward and honest about their intentions, what they're looking for and who they are, it would make online dating so much easier. Most of it is entirely about sex; no matter what anybody says, there are very few in this world who go online looking for an actual committed relationship. If they do, they either have high standards like mine, or they're so superficial, they have been on dating apps for at least a decade. From what I've experienced, most of the human race is evil, using one another as stepping stones to get what they want out of life, no matter how much it might hurt someone along the way.

My journey started blind, and I have been in several relationships since I came out, both short and long-term. The journey so far has included becoming engaged to three of my exes - once I proposed to him and the other times I was proposed to. Each time, I broke the engagement, because each one was for the wrong reasons. I had only accepted to feel a sense of comfort and familiarity. As I look back, I was settling, and never truly in love with any of them. You shouldn't be married if your whole heart isn't in it, no matter what. It's unfair to everyone concerned. As for the men I have had relationships with: I have loved things about them, but I can genuinely say I have not been in love with them so deeply that it hurts when I'm without them. Since coming out, I have been in long-term relationships of up to four years. Things always seem okay while you are in a relationship, but when you step out of it and look back, you see things differently. When I look back, none of my relationships have been true love, and what passed for love was false, or faded fast.

Even when the passion faded, I tended to stay, in hopes that it would get better. Now, when love is gone, it's gone. I haven't truly been in love with anyone as of yet, and maybe no one has ever been in love with me. As I get older, fears about certain things come more into focus. When I lie alone in bed at night, I can't help but feel that maybe I should have stayed with some of my exes, if only to have the comfort of someone being there. The problem is, I was more lonely in my relationships than I am being single.

It's hard not to wish that someone was here to tell me everything will be alright, and to know that when I am gone, I will not be forgotten. I never imagined that heading blindly into my new journey would lead to further days of heartache and sadness. Life will always continue to surprise you.

APRIL 27, 1982

. . . .

CHAPTER 3

"The two most important days in your life
are the day you are born and
the day you find out why."
~Mark Twain

What can I say? I certainly was an asshole child growing up! The chaos I caused as a kid, because of my feelings that I was not getting the attention I wanted or needed, was pretty fierce. My father, Henry, was hardly in the picture growing up. He was "home" maybe ten percent of the time, and usually, that was only because he needed something. At the time, I may have been young, but it wasn't hard to understand that he was only in need of money or a place to live when he was around. My mother, Katharine, worked, and had two kids to take care of on her own, for the most part, with some support from family. For many years my mother was a punching bag for all of my anger; I had to blame someone for my father not being around, so who better than my mom? I punished her for not doing enough to keep him home, because I thought it was her fault that he was always leaving. To me, at such a young age, I figured she must have been mistreating my dad, and that is why he left and never really came home to see us. In my mind, he was never around because he was not allowed, when, in reality, it was his choice. It took me a long time to grow and mature enough to see the truth. It only took me nearly two decades, and becoming a parent myself, to learn that truth.

Now, when I look back at that time in my life, I regret what I put her through. As an adult, I certainly appreciate the mother I was given, and all she did for my sister, Julia, and me. Just like a deadbeat father, she could have thrown her hands up in the air and walked away from it all, either leaving us behind with family, or with Child Services. My mother was only sixteen when she had my sister, and nineteen when she had me. At that young age, she had to raise us with the absence of our father for the most part. Even though she made mistakes, she was young, and I'm sure she didn't know any better, the same way I didn't know much when I started having kids. As with all parents, mistakes are made, and the child may not remember them. If remembered, the memory is clouded with a child's perception.

My parents started their lives together by marrying in May 1979, mainly due to religious factors. Our family is Catholic, and at the time, my maternal grandparents were devout followers, so my grandfather insisted on marriage. When my mother was sixteen and pregnant, she didn't get a spot on a reality TV show. Instead, all she got was a husband. My father is just two years older than my mother. They were both still kids when they started having their family, and like many others, mine came with dysfunction and judgment. Religion was never a part of my paternal grandmother, Judy's, life, although she judges everyone who comes across her path. My paternal grandfather has never been in the picture as far back as I can remember. The last thing I had heard about him was years ago, and that was to inform me that he was still alive.

Grandma Judy didn't trust my mother; she refused to attend my parent's wedding. She believed my maternal grandparents had somehow brainwashed my father. She also didn't believe her son was my (or my sister's) biological father. Well, she had that backwards; he was the biological father, but not a dad. My maternal grandparents have always had my respect, and up until a certain point in my life, I respected Judy, too. This respect lasted until I started to see how toxic she is as a person, and since around 2017, our relationship has been nil. She is a creator of great stories to make herself look good, rather than owning her mistakes. My memories are vague from the first five years of my life, but I remember some moments very clearly. There are also stories passed along from the family. My parents' dysfunctional relationship, and the events that happened before and after I was born, would seem unbelievable had I never known my father. It is unfortunate that one person's actions could create so much negativity in my family. Based on the accounts of several family members, this is how my life, from the womb onward, began:

It did not come as a surprise to my mother when she discovered she was pregnant with me in October, 1981, but it did come as a shock to Henry - he was unaware of my mother's desire for another child. Henry was young, and in a baseball league, so typically, he was not very bright regarding his hormones. At the start of July 1981, my father had a baseball game in Paris, Ontario, and my mother went along with him. After a game one night, my mother and father decided to have sex on third base. At least, I guess they decided: they may simply have tripped on the way to home, finishing the job on the third. So, my mother got what she wanted on that baseball diamond, and my father was blind to it, until her pregnancy was confirmed in the third month. Not only did my father have his age against him, but he suffered from a lack of maturity, and he was heavily into drinking and gambling.

I remember the drinking up until the last time he fell backwards through the glass sliding shower doors; it happened twice. The second time, he was taking a pee, drunk, standing at the toilet, and right back through the glass doors he fell. I was all of four years old when that happened, but I vividly remember my mom plucking glass pieces out of his back with tweezers. Afterwards, she sent him to the hospital, by ambulance, by himself. His drinking may have slowed after those early years, but back when my mother found out that she was pregnant with me, he was still enjoying his alcohol. My father was not happy to be having another child. When my mother was in her fourth month of pregnancy, she and my father got into a fight. Henry, in his rage, threw my mother up against the wall, and began to punch her in the stomach, exclaiming how he wished she would lose the baby, and that it probably wasn't his anyway.

People talk shit at times about gay men not being real fathers, yet men can beat their wives and still be praised for being "real men." My mother was not allowed to go to the hospital to be examined to make sure everything was okay, but thankfully, she didn't miscarry due to his behavior. Maybe it was my already-blooming stubbornness from the ginger hair, fighting for my place in this world. Even in the womb, I wanted what I wanted, I guess. During my mother's pregnancy, she gained over sixty pounds, even though she loved her pregnancy "diet", which consisted mainly of salad and pickles. This is most likely where I get my love of salty foods - from all those damn pickles. My mother's due date was at the start of April, but I didn't want to come out into a cruel world, I guess. They couldn't even induce labor with caster oil - my senses must have picked up that I would have an asshole for a father. So I opted to

stay in the womb, where I had endless pickles, and a safe
space.

Finally, on an early spring morning, around 5 a.m., my
mother's water broke, and she went into labor. This wasn't
a shock to my mother; she had spent the night feeling
unsettled since dinner. Henry had been drinking all night,
and was too drunk to take my mother to the hospital. Judy
drove my mother, AND her drunken son, to the hospital.
The day I was born was overly mild, close to 60°F and
sunny, slightly milder than average for that time of year. My
mother's labor was extremely short, and I came crashing
into the world just over two hours after the contractions
began. My chunky, ginger self was welcomed into
existence at 7:28 am, on April 27, 1982, weighing 9 pounds
and 9 ounces.

How welcomed I was by my father is genuinely
unknown, but he sure did celebrate my birth with the father
of twins, who were born the same day. He and the other
father were drinking and "celebrating" even before my
arrival. They were getting so loud and rowdy, that the
nurses had to ask them both to leave the room. After my
quick delivery, my father was asked if he wanted to cut the
umbilical cord, but he was too drunk to reply. He was asked
again, and he still didn't reply, so the doctor just cut the
cord, as my father sat there in silence. Of course, it was only
natural to continue to deny that I was his child after I was
born. When Henry saw that I had ginger hair, he warned my
mother that it better be blood on my head, and not red

hair. My uncles on my paternal side are ginger, and my father also has areas of ginger hair, but because I was ginger, I couldn't be his child. It seems my father has always had excuses to try and get out of his responsibilities. This is probably why I have such hatred for people who make excuses, rather than accept life's challenges as they come along.

The cutest part of the story is when my two and a half-year-old sister was given the pretend opportunity to name me. I wonder what I would have been named, four decades ago, by a toddler? The name my parents wanted to give me was Jackson, but Judy struck again with her racism. She told my parents that they couldn't give their child a black person's name. The backup plan was to name me after the doctor who delivered me, so I became James, even though I think I would have rocked the name, Jackson. Not only would I have rocked the shit out of that name, but it would also have pissed off my racist grandmother every time she had to say it. Karma, Judy, Karma! Judy is still alive, and still very racist. The way she would talk about people of a different race or group when I was growing up would make you sick; nothing but a bigot and a racist.

After my birth, my mother was kept in the hospital for five days, which was standard after delivery back in the 1980s, plus she had to have an episiotomy, which she will never let me live down. The number of times I've heard her crack the joke, "They had to cut me from one end to the other for you!" Coming home from the hospital with a new baby boy would be a happy day for most people. However, my father never arrived to pick us up. On that day he was too busy golfing, gambling, and drinking. Since my father didn't show up, and was unreachable, my mother called her parents, and they came to pick her up instead. After that, my mother decided we should stay at my maternal grandparent's home. Who knows what excuses Henry had? When he finally arrived from his day's adventures, those excuses must have worked, because my parents ended up staying together. The relationship between them was on and off, and even when it was on, he wasn't there most of the time for his family, so it would have been better to have just been off the whole time.

Henry's inability to be a father, I think, was the cause of two things:

1. It made me act like such an asshole as a child, mainly towards my mother. I was often chased around the outside of the house with some form of wooden kitchen cooking utensil, that would end up breaking over me when I was hit with it. I was always doing something wrong or mischievous.

2. Even though, in the eyes of society, I was too young to be a father, I believe my dad's unfortunate parenting model gave me the determination to never end up like him. Because I was so young, most people thought it was fucked up that Connie and I

planned our children, but this didn't hit me until many challenges later. No matter what, I could do this! I was not going to give up and walk away when things got tough, as my father had done.

So, I should thank my dad for giving me the drive to not be a lousy excuse for a father.

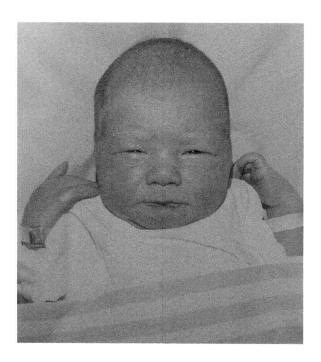

*April 27, 1982 - Hours after I was
pushed out into this cruel world.*

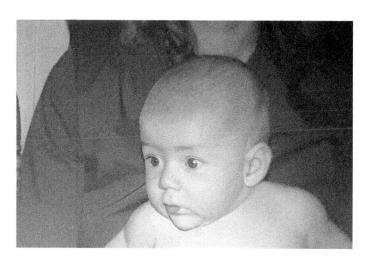

Only weeks old, and I had the look of WTF?

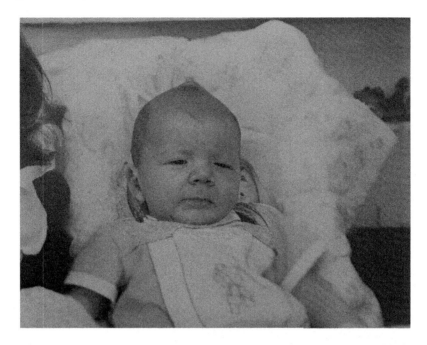

Spring 1982 - Still unsure of this world.

Late 1982 - My first Christmas!

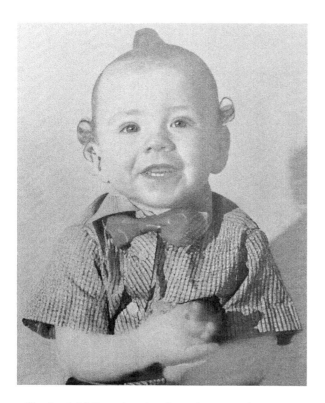

Early 1983 - I looked so happy, but I really hated that bowtie!

June 2011 - Pride, drunk and stupid!

July 2010 - My heaviest weight 314 pounds.

June 2011 - Me after my 127 pound weight loss.

Though I grew up without my father for the vast majority of my life, I did have many people who were there for me, who cared for and loved me, no matter how much of an ass I was. My maternal grandparents were always there for me, and I spent much time at their house while growing up. Most of the fatherly things I've learned in life, I learned from my grandfather. He would take me on fishing trips, to roadshows, and he would even take me to work with him. We would have early morning coffee runs, and even though I never liked hockey, I would always go to any games when asked, because I loved the time I spent with him. I developed a great love for cooking from my grandmother. She was always cooking from scratch, and one of the best things in the world was to walk into their home, smelling her home-cooked meals.

Judy was also there a few times a year, to take my sister and me for a week or so, to her place in Toronto, Ontario. I certainly can't say she was the best role model, but there are some good memories with her, growing up. She baked, and my sister and I always looked forward to her homemade cookies. Judy would send us home with tins of cookies, but the next time we saw her, she would tell us we were fat. She hated fat people, and she certainly didn't discriminate against ANY groups of people who were "different." In short, she was a bigot. If my sister and I went for a visit, and Julia or I had gained weight, she would lecture us, and then offer us a cash incentive for each pound we could lose. This happened well before we were even teenagers. She would feed us and then fatten us up like veal, only to later make us feel guilty for the weight. #grandparentinggoals

My family also included aunts and uncles who were there for me if I needed them, along with cousins to play with. My mom had a best friend that I still speak with on occasion. She even lives in the same town as I do now. She is a lesbian, and has been my whole life. As a kid, whenever I would see her, she would lift me by my ankles and bite my ass, hard. Man, I was not too fond of it then, but the memories are priceless, and will last forever. Imagine the uproar if someone were to say that was happening to them in this day and age. Shit! Watch out! The keyboard warriors would be out in full swing, calling for an arrest for child abuse. I can't imagine my life without all of my experiences, good or bad. I can't imagine who I would have become without them, or without the people I had in my life.

Maybe if Judy weren't such a racist nasty person, I wouldn't have seen what racism looks like. There is good in almost all circumstances, if you look at the big picture. It may have been only a small fraction of my childhood, but at least something good came out of it. Each day is different, and now, when I find it hard to find anything positive, a reminder may be needed from my best friend, that today is just one day. Tomorrow is always a new day, and we may see the world in a whole different light.

If I were to sum up my life in one sentence, it would have to be "Causing havoc and trying to do right since 1982."

DEAR, DAD

....

CHAPTER 4

"My dad broke my heart way before any boy had a chance to."

Parenting is never done. All you do is worry about what can happen, whether it's at three weeks gestation into the pregnancy or twenty-five years old. Starting a family might seem to be an inspired, beautiful idea - after all it's human nature - but most people only see the contended, happy facade before jumping in. It is incredible having kids - they're the only complete true love you will ever have in life. At least they should be. Many couples seem to have created the perfect little package; a delightful family unit, with Mom, Dad, and kids, all living happily together.

However, so many people fail to see the blatant truth; that it's hard as fuck to be a parent. Being an involved parent every single day is the most demanding job imaginable. Part of the population will say to stay-at-home parents, "You have it easy!" Okay, sure, some days may be much easier than others, but if you haven't raised a child, you haven't gone through those gut-wrenching worries and scares, followed by extreme relief, all within a span of sixty-seconds. As a parent, you will understand what I mean by that. Before deciding to get pregnant, be sure you're ready to be a parent. Realize that your life will no longer be about you. From the moment that test comes back positive, life will never be the same. Ever!

My father, Henry, was only twenty-one years old when I was born. He was in, maybe, ten percent of my life when I was a kid, and almost zero percent as an adult. Once I came out as gay to him, he said that I just needed a good night out at Hooters sports bar or the strip club. My reply was around the lines of "You can put all the tit in my face that you want, but I will just want their boyfriends/husbands, not them." He also asked me how I would know I was gay if I hadn't had sex with a guy yet. His question was valid, because I hadn't even kissed a guy at that point. The response I gave him was the same as I would tell anyone, "How did you know you were attracted to or wanted to have sex with women?" He stopped and somewhat shrugged his shoulders, and was like, "I just knew!" To which I replied, "Exactly, you just know!" It was with a bit of a huff and puff that he left the room. That was it; he has never spoken another word about my sexuality to my face.

Since coming out, I have seen my father approximately five times. One of those times, Julia brought him to my business. When he came in, he was polite to my staff, said hello to them, and then proceeded to ignore me by not saying a single word. It hurt. Not only did I feel the pain of his not being there for most of my childhood, but then he made it worse by using my coming out as a valid reason (in his eyes) not to interact with me or my children. He was and is a selfish, self-centered man, and I don't think that will change, even on his deathbed.

I wrote this letter to Henry so I could start to heal, and to let go of some of the pain and anger he has caused.

Dear Dad,

I don't think I know you well enough to honestly say I love you. You have never given me the chance to be your son and show you who I am. As far back as my memory will take me, you have never been there for me, let alone even been a dad to me for more than a couple of months at a time. Even when you came back home, it was just for your own selfish needs. It didn't take very long for me to realize that you weren't here for the family. You came back because you had burned through all of your bridges, and had nowhere else to go. For so much of my childhood, I watched you come and go whenever it suited your fucking needs. My anger is not from your coming and going in my life. It's because of what you didn't do during those short visits. You never did anything to try and be my dad. When you weren't there, you weren't there: you never even called on birthdays or holidays. If I received a birthday card, it wasn't really from you. It was from mom, or from some woman you were dating, and they would sign your name. I remember, when I was seven or eight years old, you came to play catch in the backyard with one of my friends and me. This was rare; one of the very few moments I can remember you trying to do anything "dadlike" with me. During what was supposed to be a father-son moment in the yard, I got hit in the face with the baseball.

Do you remember that? When the tears started to roll from my eyes and I went inside the house, you dismissed it. You wanted me to "man up," stop the crying, go back outside, and continue to play catch. On those rare occasions we did things together, they were always things you liked; never things I wanted to do. My memories of you are minimal, and they are mostly of you being a fucking asshole. It was always about you. If (perish the thought), it wasn't about you, it was because it was forced by the woman you were dating at that time. If it were up to you, you wouldn't have ever been there for anything. You would rather be gambling what money you had, or what you could scam and take from others.

It has been about nine years since I interacted with you, and about five years since you ignored me in my place of business. A moment that stands out for me was the Thanksgiving dinner your girlfriend planned one year. I had already come out, and you were still somewhat around. When you found out that my male partner and I would be invited to dinner, you told your girlfriend that if I was going to be there, you weren't. It became a holiday that I couldn't be a part of, because of your pig-headed way of thinking, and your selfish tantrums: you would leave if you didn't get what you wanted. Fuck you! That is what I have to say, Henry.

What few moments I could have had with you as father and son were destroyed, because you are such an asshole. I wasn't invited that year or any year that followed. You forced your hand, encouraging others to profess the same hate as yours; to listen to and be a part of the lies, because you think gay men are nothing but whores, sluts, and disgusting humans who shouldn't even exist. A woman eating another woman's pussy every night of the week is hawt, but your son loving another man is wrong. You may think I'm disgusting, but Henry, turn around and look in the mirror. You should be disgusted with yourself. You're a pathetic piece of shit, and a sorry excuse for a man.

Sitting here as I write this, I can't help but think to myself, what have you done in your life that has been for the benefit of others? Only you, Henry, really know the answer to that question. You have caused rifts in the immediate family, too many times to count. You put Julia's marriage in jeopardy when you couldn't find a place to live, and you had to stay with her - yet again. It didn't even seem to bother you that you were once again disrupting an actual family, but then, what would you know about true family, right, Henry? You gambled away family money, risking people's financial security, but did that matter to you? Of course not!

In the more than nine years since we last conversed with one another, I have seen you once at my place of business, and you said nothing to me, but you did say hello to my staff and introduced yourself as Henry. Rude! Just plain rude! If you can come inside the business that I built to take care of my family, you can, at the very least, swallow your fucking ego and say hello to your son. People have always said I need to try and make amends with you, and I always say you can't make amends with someone who only sees things one way, and most likely always will. You don't deserve to be in my life or your grandchildren's lives. When I started my family with Connie, who was thirteen years my senior, you weren't there. When I married Connie, you came to my wedding because your girlfriend forced you to show up.

Remember standing up at my wedding reception to make your speech? I sure do! You stood up and said that you were proud of me. Fucking funny way, Henry, of showing the "pride" you said you have for your son. The only thing that has changed since then is who I love as a partner in life. Let's talk about Henry's partners. Remember the situation I had to defuse, when a friend of mine and Connie's saw her "happily married neighbor" at my wedding with my father? You brought your girlfriend, who was cheating on her husband, to my wedding! And the funniest part was that your girlfriend was the one who *forced you to come to my wedding in the first place. This woman was married, living with her husband and kids while seeing you, and SHE was the one that had to get my own father to attend my wedding.*

I don't feel sorry for the life you have created, and you deserve all the misery you have caused yourself in life. Living in and out of hotels, back stretches of race tracks, in random women's homes, and so forth. It's interesting that, never once since I've known you, have you ever had your own apartment or house. You've had your own motel room, or a room at the race track; all great places for your kids to visit, right? Oh wait, that's right - you never wanted visits. How sad it is that you have had nothing to offer anyone but grief and heartache. Henry, I have so much anger towards you. For all of those wasted years, I simply needed a father. I needed love - from you and for you.

When Mom was pregnant, you were borderline alcoholic. You accused her of cheating and held her against the wall, punching her in the stomach. You told her you wished she would lose the baby. Well, I wish she had cheated on you and that you weren't my father; I guess neither of us got what we wanted. Maybe if she had cheated, I would have gotten a biological father to turn to, and have a relationship with. When I was born, many have said that your words when you saw me were, "That better be blood on his head!" This, of course, is about me having red hair. These stories weren't told to me just by Mom. I have heard them from multiple family members, who are all fine and well; thanks for asking.

Growing up, I used to always try and stick up for you, in hopes that maybe I would get your attention and love. All it did was get you what you needed, and nothing else. You're almost sixty-one years old, and I think that I have had you in my life for maybe three years combined, if I were to add them up. What kind of role model are you for anyone, except perhaps someone on www.ashleymadison.com? When do you man up and become a productive part of society? When you retire, what do you retire from? Living off others?

Henry, I am me, and you're a part of me, no matter what, but your actions, or lack of them, have created the walls and barriers I have today. If it weren't for you and Mom, I wouldn't be here, or if Mom had chosen someone else, I would most likely be a completely different person. However, like always, you needed your gratification, so you had sex on third base and created me; your (in your eyes) disappointing and disgusting son.

Henry, I can go to my grave without regretting never speaking to nor seeing you again. People say I will regret that choice, but they didn't have to live the life I did with you as my father. Henry, when I hear of your passing one day, I will make sure to do something in your honor. I will honor you by doing the same as you would, by not being there for you, and not showing up. I will not attend your funeral, and I will not mourn your death. I have already mourned your absence for many long years. Now it's time to move forward, without the weight of all the hate and sadness towards you on my shoulders. I can now do just that - with the peace of mind and solace I have gained through this letter to you. Currently, there is nothing left to do or say, except something you rarely did for me:

Happy Birthday, Dad!
Happy Easter, Dad!
Happy Father's Day, Dad!
Happy Thanksgiving, Dad!
Merry Christmas, Dad!
Happy New Year's, Dad!

With disgust,
James

P.S. Henry, you may not be here to show me or tell me how you feel about my life, but many others are, and they're just like you. Almost daily, I am reminded of what I am in the eyes of others.

I'm pathetic.
I'm a f*g.
I need Jesus, no if's, and's, or "butts" about it, I need Jesus.
I'm a sad individual.

I'm super fucking gay.
I need to jump off a bridge and die.

So, no worries, Henry, the other homophobes in your clan
got your back.

When you become a parent, you give up the freedom to do what you want for most of your kid's childhood. Whether you're male or female, if you're not ready to give your attention and care to someone other than yourself, practice safe sex. Once you have children, it's your responsibility to be there and take care of them. It has always bothered me, perhaps more than others, to see people who cannot take responsibility for their actions. Hearing women trash men and call them "deadbeat" dads is infuriating, because I see almost equal numbers of "deadbeat" mothers out there.

Unlike my dad, who was never there for me, I stayed for my kids. No matter how many times I hear people talk shit about me, I just shake my head, and wonder if they critique their own life the way they do mine. Since coming out in 2011, my children have been with me over 80% of the time. The little money I have made has gone towards providing what I could for them. Shit, I could have come out and done what my father did to me - just fuck off and only return when I needed something. A lot of people who know of me only online have put their two cents in, with comments about how I probably just fucked off and left my family, never see my kids, and just have gay sex and do drugs. Comments of this type pop up frequently.

I like to think that, even though I may not have had a lot materially to offer my kids, I at least did a decent job staying and providing as best I could. I'm not angry about my choices, but I did give up my youth for my children. This is a choice that I made in life, and I love my kids. My sexuality could never change my love for my children, and they are my responsibility. I may not love their mother like I once did; that never meant I would walk away from it all. I have made many mistakes in my life, and many of them have been as a father. It's hard not to wonder if my children would have had a better life, had I made some different decisions and choices in life. These are the same thoughts I have about my dad.

What if he had stayed? Would I be the person I am today, or would I still be the closeted adult, afraid of my dad, scared to be who I truly am? Of course, these are questions that have no answers. Yup, there will be many people reading this who will start going on with their opinions about how, if my dad had been around, I wouldn't be gay, and if I weren't gay, then my kids would have had a better life and so on. I do have to say: if those are your thoughts - stick it! Unless you have lived it, you have no right to judge it.

Out of all of the pain and anger that I feel towards my father, I hope my kids aren't holding on to that kind of pain, hate, resentment, or anger towards me. If they are, I hope they talk to me about it. I am always here for them, and will listen to what they have to say. My kids live with me, so I hope that's a sign that they don't hold anywhere near the pain that I do for my father. I would gladly take it on for them, rather than allow it to darken their childhood memories, and turn them into troubled adults. If I ever received a "Dear, Dad" letter, I would make sure to address everything in it to the best of my ability. You can only begin to heal once you allow yourself to accept and let go of the hurt. People, including myself, have had some pretty heavy shit to deal with in their lives, and if I could say one thing to anyone going through something serious, it would be, don't be afraid to get help. In my experience, too many people are scared to talk or seek out a psychotherapist or counselor. Don't be! They're a great resource. Take the help if it's available to you.

Don't allow someone else's misery and negativity to take away your happiness. If you have a parent in your life like my father, know that no matter what, you're loved. It may not be someone you expect, but you're loved. Sometimes we don't see it, especially when we feel down and low about ourselves. This is because of the way people have made us feel in the past. We all have made mistakes, including my douche canoe of a father. Still, you are the only one who can redeem yourself, and it starts with finding and loving yourself. Then, you can begin to forgive yourself, and ask for forgiveness for your wrongdoings. I know that, between my dad's absence from my life, and the lack of a partner's love, I can't help but sometimes feel that the people who criticize me for my lifestyle may actually be right. But, this is in no way true. No matter your sexuality, you will feel a sense of loss and loneliness at some point. Some of the loneliest times in my life were when I was in a relationship with someone, and I believe this was due to my lack of love for myself. Because of that, I settled for individuals I thought would love me, and help fill that void, but it didn't.

My "Dear, Dad" letter was for my own benefit. In the course of our lives, people will hurt us, whether it be accidentally or on purpose. How we handle it will show how, or if, we recover from the pain it caused. Will I forget or forgive what my father did or didn't do for me growing up? Probably not! But, I can get past it, if I understand that there is nothing I can do to change the past. I had to let go and move forward. It doesn't mean that I have to forget in order to forgive what my father did to me. Perhaps my father doesn't think he is at fault. I don't know that answer; only he does. Let's face it, though: he knew what he was doing, and it would be ignorant to pretend he isn't aware of the ramifications of his choices.

In my experience, feeling low about ourselves comes from negative experiences, whether with family or relationships. Don't let other people's poor self-esteem, narrow-mindedness, and negativity destroy your view of yourself, or keep you from accepting yourself. We're all broken; some of us are just better at pretending. Those who trash other's lifestyles usually do so because of their own unhappiness. Seeing people do what makes them happy bothers them, because they feel stuck, and haven't "found their way." The people behind the closed doors of those perfect, white-picket-fence houses, who appear picture-perfect, are miserable, and some even closeted alcoholics. Maybe husband and wife don't communicate anymore. Maybe they just no longer care. Maybe bitterness is making them die inside, a little more each day. They know they're unhappy, but they don't know what to do about it. So, for whatever reason, they stay, creating a living hell for themselves, and anyone with them. One can't hold such tremendous unhappiness and stress inside, and not expect it to impact family and loved ones.

Every person's view of beauty is different; we all find different things attractive in life. We may not love our face, ears, hands, body, etc., but there are people in this world who love and admire those qualities about you. Take care of and love yourself, and you will find true happiness.

Dear My Beautiful Readers,

Beauty begins the moment you decide to be yourself!

Remember,

You're Loved!
You're Beautiful!
No Matter What Anyone Says!

Love and Hugs,
James

SEXUALITY UNKNOWN

. . . .

CHAPTER 5

*"You don't forget the day you lose yourself,
but the day you rediscover
yourself is miraculous."*

Recalling childhood memories, I can now say with confidence that I had more feelings of a homosexual nature than a heterosexual one. My school years were like the opening scene of a popular teen show, with a closeted gay male lead. As it starts, you think you "know," but after an episode or two, you "know" he is into guys, and that he will soon be slurping on a dick and not motor-boating a pussy. During my childhood, I remember, not so much of my sexuality, as just being different. I attributed this to the fact that I was a poor, chubby, freckled ginger. My sexual attractions started about the time I entered high school. In P.E. I had to avoid the locker rooms: I didn't want to get a boner changing with the other guys. I think this was also when I fell in love with the scent of, "male musk." During this period, my body didn't seem to know what was happening, and my mind didn't have a clue, either.

Most of my best friendships were with females - I found them beautiful and fun to be around. Looking back on those days, I don't think there was ever an attraction to females in a sexual way. I recall being extremely shy around most males of any age, but feeling really comfortable with girls. At the time, I thought these were normal feelings, common to all young boys. So far as I knew, I was just a typical, curious kid; a bit mischievous and testing the rules and boundaries whenever possible.

My journey to adulthood has taught me so much, but there is one thing I want parents to take away from it. As humans, we are all sexual beings, and no matter where we are in our lives, we feel and see different things that arouse sexual curiosity. Being a parent myself, I ask that other parents talk to their children from early school age and up about sexuality. I'm not suggesting you start with the whole "birds and bees" talk, but, for your child's well-being, I recommend that you speak to them about age-appropriate feelings. Let your children know that it's okay to love another human, no matter what their gender may be. Speak to them about healthy ways to express their feelings, even letting them know that it's normal to feel an attraction to males, females, or both, and that as they grow, they will discover who they are.

By having these ongoing conversations throughout their childhood, you are also building healthy bridges of communication. These bridges will help your child feel comfortable coming to you to talk and ask questions. Please do your part to help your kids understand that, no matter who they love, or who they want to be in life, it's completely normal and acceptable. Let them grow up knowing you will always have their backs. Remember, love starts at home-but so does hate.

My first experience with a vagina was an absolute horror show. I was only five years old, but I remember it vividly. I was attending kindergarten at a local public school, and pussy got me in trouble without even having to touch it. Our classroom was at the back of the school, with a second classroom door leading out into the back schoolyard. Since we were only in kindergarten, and didn't have the best control of our small bladders, we had a washroom of our own, located by the door coming in from the schoolyard. It was a single washroom, with just one bathroom stall. How I wish there had been boys and girls restrooms, instead of a single stall, shared by the class.

On that sweltering summer day, my classmates and I were running around, playing outside in the schoolyard, with the back door propped open to let air inside the stifling classroom. I knew I had to pee, but I ended up waiting too long, letting it become urgent - so urgent that I was doing a little Criss Cross Potty dance. I ran to my teacher, Mrs. Thatcher, to get permission to go to the washroom. She said yes, not realizing that my classmate, a girl named Gina, was already in there. I scurried quickly into the classroom, flung open the bathroom door, and to my surprise, as well as hers, there was Gina, just standing there.

We locked eyes in shock, and within those few seconds, she lifted her sundress up high, with her underwear still at her ankles. Gina began to flaunt her vagina with a bit of sway in her hips like she was waving a flag. I was horrified! I knew it was wrong to be looking at someone's private parts, but I didn't know how to react to what I was seeing. There stood Gina with her dress basically over her head and her "Cookie" (or, in my mind, "Cookie Monster") exposed to the wind. Mortified, I swear I almost pissed my pants right there. Boys were always the bad ones who caused trouble, or so it seemed in school. Shit, I knew I was done for.

Seeing Gina's female bits, by no choice of my own, was going to end up being my fault. Boy, was I right! She put down her dress and ran out the classroom door just as another classmate, Jacob, came inside. Gina ran out of the back door, yelling so loudly, I could hear her from inside the classroom - "Mrs. Thatcher, James opened that bathroom door so he could peek at me!" My face was hot, I was so upset being blamed for something that she did on purpose. When a five-year-old boy has to pee SO bad, and the bathroom door isn't locked, you're going to go in. Yes, of course, I should have knocked first to make sure no one was in the stall, but even so, I did not make her pull her sundress up to expose her vagina. But, I was a boy, so I got the blame. Not even five years old, and a vagina already had me in hot water. That was certainly one way to keep me from wanting to look at or touch a female's treasure chest, that's for sure.

Throughout childhood I was curious about sex and sexuality, but my access to reliable information and examples was limited. I was always taught that boys are supposed to like girls, and girls are supposed to like boys - at least that was the way I perceived it. Any relationship other than, "one man/one woman," was frowned upon, and in a world already so full of hate and cruelty, I was afraid any deviations would make me an even bigger social outcast. Growing up in the '80s and '90s wasn't easy, but it was exponentially harder for a poor, chubby, freckled-faced ginger. I was one of those kids who was constantly bullied in school. Schoolmates already called me names like f*g, homo, or even plain ole "gay" daily. This started when I was about seven years old. It scared me because those words weren't being said in jest. They were meant to be mean and hurtful.

Even though these were terrific years for big names, such as Prince, Elton John, and Michael Jackson, there was so much homophobia concerning gay celebrities and those whose sexuality was considered questionable. Growing up seeing and hearing people poke fun at Michael Jackson, because they believed he was homosexual, had me hoping that I was not a "homo." The things I observed as a child stuck with me, and made me want to avoid the mental torture I imagined gay people had to endure. I heard how my father, Henry (when he was around), would speak of gay men. His words left me feeling that, if I ever came out and said I had sexual feelings for another guy, I would end up being a disappointment, and disowned for life. The thought of that killed me. Even though he wasn't there for me much growing up, it still hurt knowing that, if that's who I was, it would have to be hidden.

Henry always seemed to favor my sister, Julia; when he was around, they did everything together. This was through no fault of hers; it was just really shitty parenting on his part. When my dad was around, I heard homophobic remarks about gay men from him, though he never had any issues with lesbians (like many straight men, I guess). The fear of not fitting in in this world was so hard to take, that I mostly kept to myself. Being made fun of by schoolmates and friends of my sister for stupid things, like having a softer voice, acting too "feminine", or not having much body hair, had me dying on the inside. I just wanted to be "normal". I didn't see anything wrong with myself until the taunting started. As the negativity continued, I began to believe it. I didn't want to live in a world of fear, so I guess I decided to live in the shadows. I told myself that all my thoughts and feelings were simply a "phase" I was going through and I would outgrow it once puberty was done kicking the crap out of me.

Meanwhile, girls always seemed to cause me grief. When I was about seven, a girl from school invited me over for a play date at her house. Her parents were in the living room; they were very polite and introduced themselves to me. Her bedroom door was right off of the living room, where they were sitting. We went into her room to play, and she closed the door. Once the door closed, I remember her saying the words "Wanna fuck"? I was mortified, and didn't know what to do or say at that moment. Panic set in. I stumbled over my words, saying things like, "But your parents are in the living room." She replied "That's fine; they won't come in here. Trust me, I do this all the time." She was so set on doing it, like this was a daily thing for her, and she was only a year older than me! I just kept repeating, "I don't think we should, I don't want to get caught", while in my head, I was thinking that I didn't want to touch her pussy or "Hershey Kisses" size tits. After about thirty minutes, I made an excuse, saying I was expected home for dinner. I left as quickly as possible, ignoring her asking me to come back later. Never did I return to her house or even speak to her again.

No matter how many days, months, or years pass, I can count on one hand the number of times I had sexual fantasies about a female. The times I did, to my recollection, it felt as though I was forcing them, just wanting to be normal. Once, I remember fantasizing about a female friend that I liked, and thought was pretty, while trying to masturbate. In the end, I was so raw I couldn't complete my mission at all, and I felt sick and freakish, being unable to jerk off while thinking about a girl. I had non-sexual crushes on girls early on, from around the age of six, but they weren't anything but bonding with girls who were nice to me, and not mean like others. But at about the same time, I was also starting to have a crush on the boy who lived across the street from us; his name was Conner. Conner's mother, Bonnie, hated me with every bone in her body - probably in just the same way I disliked her.

Along with my newfound crushes, I began to have fantasies about boys, and what it would be like to touch another boy's trouser snake. Now, these fantasies were coming in by the dozens, if not hundreds. Shame and guilt were familiar feelings I would have when I thought a guy was attractive, or I was having sexual fantasies about him. Multiple times in my early teens, I would start to fantasize about what it would be like if I gave into my ever-increasing attraction to boys. When I let my mind wander into the danger zone of erotic daydreams, I would get an enormous knot of guilt in my stomach. I wasn't supposed to be feeling this way, and I couldn't be a "homo." It wasn't right.

Yet all I wanted to do was experiment, to see if I was really into boys exclusively, or just attracted to their looks.

Before letting my curiosity win, I would be overcome by the shadow of shame and guilt. Often, while hanging out with my male friends, I would lose my train of thought from the distraction of being more and more sexually attracted to them. In retrospect, I'm pretty sure some of them had mutual feelings, but they didn't act on them, although there were times when I would be a bit more "ballsy" and test the gay waters. The more I did, the more I began to think that I liked the flavor of that water. The guts and desire to taste those waters came a couple of years after the restroom incident with Gina. His name was Luis.

Luis and I became the best of friends, and there was nothing we didn't do together. We were typical, mischievous boys - playing in the dirt, lighting things on fire, melting whatever wouldn't burn, and having sleepovers almost every weekend. Luis was an adorable boy. He had dark chestnut brown hair, big brown eyes, a sandy complexion, and he was a pretty rugged kid. He liked getting dirty, and pulling things apart to examine how they worked. Luis always had scrapes and bruises from his adventures outside or in, tearing things apart. He was what most people would call a typical boy's boy, and I loved that.

Usually, our sleepovers started with playing outside, only coming indoors when the street lights came on. When we were inside, we would almost always go to his room and play with his toys or melt crayons with light bulbs (perhaps this was an early onset of a fetish for one or both of us - you know wax is big in kink). Once it was lights out and bedtime, things would become a bit more interesting. Luis and I would generally cuddle; well, mostly touching and rubbing each other down. Neither one of us seemed to be ashamed about what we were doing, and to me, it was simple curiosity: just two friends touching each other's dingles to see if they were the same. In conclusion, it was pretty much like comparing apples to apples, except Luis's had a hood warmer. That was the part that confused the shit out of me. I had never seen a penis with foreskin before. It was fascinating, but I never asked about it. I just assumed we were born with different-looking penises.

Luis and I lost touch after he moved away, and to this day, I don't know what became of him. Since he has a very generic last name, hundreds of men with his name exist. Perhaps one day, now that we have the technology, he will reach out and find me. I like to think Luis would agree that what we were doing was harmless experimentation. It couldn't have been more, because boys don't have sexual feelings for other boys, or so I thought. All I knew at the time was that my favorite part of the whole week was when I would get to lie there in bed with Luis. How could something that felt so right, be so wrong? I'm not talking about sex; I'm talking about feeling love for another boy.

Society taught me that boys don't kiss other boys, love other boys or have sex with other boys. I was young, but I did know what sex was; maybe not in complete detail, but I did know what it was. Yet, here I was, unknowingly feeling all warm and fuzzy about another boy. I may not have understood it at the time, but that was how it felt. My attraction to boys was growing, and I was beginning to have crushes on them. I believe there was love for a few along the way, as silly and odd as that may seem to most. I fell into a very sexually curious stage around the age of nine or ten. At the time, I was good friends with a boy named Caden. Caden was the son of a very prestigious and well-known family in the small town where we lived. Like my other crushes, Caden had dark chestnut brown hair. Unlike the others, however, Caden's eyes were bright blue. He had a very tanned complexion, and a smile that made my heart skip a beat. He became my best friend, and we did everything together. "Everything" included acting on our new budding sexual urges with one another.

In most respects, we were two old souls who did everything together, but then, there were times we would hide away in one of our favorite secluded areas, and hold one another in complete silence. It felt wrong, but unbelievably fantastic and right at the same time. There were days when Caden and I would lie naked together, cuddled tightly, and all we would do was talk and kiss. Other times things would become so intense, that we were unable to express our feelings with any clarity. Silently, we shared the uncertainty of what could happen if we continued this behavior. We were only children, but we knew that the world, or at least the people in OUR world, didn't condone or accept what we were doing. Sadly, these liaisons occurred infrequently, and we usually would just hang out and play in the woods: or, when the weather was crappy, we would play games indoors. There was never a shortage of things to do with Caden. He seemed to have every toy or game you could imagine. Still, the occasional days when we could lie down somewhere in private, hold each other, and talk, were the best. Looking back, that was probably some of the most honest communication I ever had in a relationship, as a child, or, as an adult. I guess the filter that so often silences grown-ups isn't fully developed at that age.

On one of those warm summer days, when we were lying outside, bodies held tightly together in a very intimate situation, his father came outside. He yelled out to Caden, telling him it was time to go inside. My heart stopped dead at that moment. We both thought we had been caught with our pants down, and that we were about to get the beating of a lifetime. This fear was justified, based on the many times I had heard Caden getting spanked by his parents. My heart broke for him whenever I heard him crying and begging for his dad to stop spanking him. Most of the time, he would come out from getting his punishment with a look of embarrassment on his face, holding his head down low.

So this day, we were sure if we got caught naked together, we would be dead by his father's hand. Before he could come and catch us, we pulled and zipped our pants up as fast as we possibly could. Moments later, Caden's dad came over, and we still had our shirts off. We told him our shirts were off because it was hot outside, and we were sweaty. His father seemed to believe our story, and we got away with it. Caden went with his father, and I booked it off the property as fast as possible, before his dad somehow figured it out. A year after that, my family moved away. I never saw Caden again. Over the last decade or so, I could have friended him on social media to connect again, but the fear of "What if this just stirs the pot?" would always take over and prevent me from doing it.

Caden is heterosexual, from what I have heard. So for him, this could have just been a childhood phase, or maybe he has yet to come to terms with his sexuality. For me, when I look back and think about it, that experience was one of the building blocks in the development of my real true love for the same sex. However, it took me many years to realize and come to terms with that. It may have been no more than a disconcerting phase for Caden, but I will never forget those summer days, when we would lie down outside somewhere, cuddled together, half undressed. Just feeling the warmth and closeness of our bodies in the silence, just being one, was amazing. I miss Caden and the relationship we once had, even though we were so young. No one ever knew about us, and I didn't act on any sexual curiosities after that for over two years.

Thinking back before Caden, when I was about eight years old, there was a cute blond-haired, blue-eyed boy named Charlie, who lived close to my grandparent's house. In the summer months, I would frequently have extended stays and visits at my maternal grandparents' home, sometimes even for the whole summer break from school. Charlie was so cute, and he was about a year or so younger than me. We shared a great love of nature, and had lots of fun playing outside in the small forest behind his house. He and I were good friends, but I wasn't attracted to him. Still, hanging out together helped me realize that I may be gay. When Charlie and I played together, it generally at some point got us in trouble. This was awesome, because we would get in shit with his stepdad. Oh, Gawd! Was his stepdad ever hawt! He was kind, sweet, handsome, had dark hair, rough hands (he was a contractor), and terrific, chiseled features.

Charlie was fun to hang out with, but I loved it when his stepdad was home, because it made the time at his house even better. If that wasn't enough to give me a clue, there was Charlie's sister. She was nineteen, and a pin-up girl model in a large city newspaper publication. She was the girl of the month, and there were pictures of her in a skimpy two-piece bikini all over the house, along with other modeling shoots that she had done. The girl was beautiful, and most boys would have jumped at the chance to go to Charlie's to see her, but I felt no sexual attraction - not to the, large breasts, long blonde hair, blue eyes, nor slim build. Most full-grown men would have been busting a nut over her, and I wanted their stepdad. Funny how I still just thought that I was a boy going through a phase, not realizing that I was gay. Sometimes you just have to live life, and let the roads guide you to your current path.

It had now been about two years since Caden, and we lost our connection to one another. We lived in a new area of town, and I was in a new school, when I met a boy named Noah. It didn't take long for Noah and I to become inseparable, and he became my new best friend. We hung out almost every single day together, and caused so much shit in the neighborhood, that there probably wasn't an adult in town who liked us. Through our many years of friendship, Noah and I did things that, had we been caught, would have gotten us grounded for life, beaten within an inch of our lives, or thrown in jail. Noah and I were bad influences on each other, but I chose to pretend it wasn't true, because I enjoyed what we were doing. Noah and I had sleepovers all the time, sometimes lasting 4 to 5 days in a row, even on school nights. During our sleepovers, we were always up late, sneaking out and walking the streets of our small town in Ontario, Canada. We would walk to the local 24 Hr coffee shop, get tea or coffee, and smoke cigarettes that we either purchased illegally or stole from his father. At this time, I was about twelve years old, and Noah was one year my senior.

On our journeys, we would vandalize property or cars. As an adult, I look back on the shit we caused, and wish I could make it right somehow. If I could go back in time, I would kick my own ass for being such a fucking mischievous little shit. We did things I am not proud of by any means, but at the time, I felt I had to keep up with my best friend, or I could risk losing him. So, together we raided gardens that people had worked hard on for months, we would snap car antennas off, pour liquid car wax into gas tanks, and we even stole lawn ornaments right off of people's front lawns. We would then dump the stolen items in another part of town, to avoid getting caught redhanded with them. Noah and I were also great at stealing items from the big box store in town. If only the word problems in math class had been about finding the total number of cassette tapes two thieves could remove from their security boxes and shove down their pants, we would have had outstanding marks, at least in mathematics. There are many regrets from that time in my life, maybe even more regrets than what I have today, but I was trying to fit in, trying not to be an outcast.

Doing these things with Noah seemed to help drown out what I was feeling on the inside. I was no longer wrong about my sexuality, just the things I was doing to other people's property. One of the reasons I stayed friends for so long with Noah, is that he never bullied me about how I acted. He never made me feel like that outcast who had a softer voice, or "feminine" qualities. Once, when I was twelve, Noah and I went on a walk, trying to find things to get into. On this particular walk, something caught our eye in a small wooded area off the main road. When we entered the area; we noticed a plastic grocery bag, discarded in a small stream. We retrieved the bag, and discovered that it was full of VHS tapes, wet from the water of the stream. One of the tapes had a weird title, and we got a monster laugh out of it. I believe it was called "Dick for Food" or something cheesy along those lines. Naturally, we took that VHS tape back to Noah's house to dry out.

We talked about watching it, but Noah wasn't sure if we should, since, judging from the title, it could be a gay porno, and Noah kept making it clear that he was straight. Actually, he was trying harder than a Southern preacher to prove his heterosexuality at that moment. So, being a lousy influence, I suggested that we watch it, and we could "pretend" that the guys in the movie were having sex with women. Even though he was a year older than me, I was a stage or two ahead of Noah in puberty, which caused him to be extremely self-conscious of his body. He eventually agreed to watch the video with me, so we put it in the VHS player, and pressed play. It was definitely a gay-themed porno. It started with a guy, just wearing short shorts and a male crop top, hitch-hiking, while holding a sign reading, "Will work for food." Naturally, a car pulls over, and a hot, ripped, sweaty, shirtless guy says to him, "Get in!" Minutes later, they arrive at a large mansion, and in the backyard, there are many men in speedos, and a buffet of foods which seemed to include unlimited "sausages" and "buns." Within seconds, the driver of the car says to the hitchhiker, "Thought you said you would work for food?" as he begins to push the hitchhiker's head down, so he can start sucking his "naturally" already erect, uncircumcised cock.

Now, Noah and I were totally interested in what was going on, but Noah claimed it would be more of a turn-on if it were women. My reply to him was, "Well, just pretend that one of the guys sucking is a woman!" After I said that, I put the offer on the table to suck his cock, just as they did in the movie. We were sitting on the lower half of the bunk beds in his bedroom, as he debated with himself about my proposal. We were completely unsupervised, but still, Noah was a bit hesitant. Finally, he decided it would be okay if we sucked each other's cock with our eyes closed, pretending that our mouth belonged to a female. Noah laid back on the bed and closed his eyes, as I began sucking on his prepubescent penis. He stopped me within seconds, saying that he was worried we could contract something from each other if we had oral sex. Being extremely naive, we thought that covering his penis with a sandwich baggie would do the trick and protect us both. Once the plastic bag was over his cock, Noah laid back down, and I resumed performing oral sex over his now sandwich baggie-covered dick. Within minutes, he orgasmed, jumped up quickly, and left the room.

Later, we agreed to destroy the tape and never speak of what took place that day, ever again. Our friendship continued as if nothing had ever happened, and he and I were still great friends. However, I was never really physically attracted to him. That afternoon of experimentation apparently satisfied a bit of sexual curiosity for both of us. Still, it left one question unanswered: Did seeing gay sex as depicted in that video, indicate that sex between men is normal, or was it a warning that I was risking burning in hell for all eternity? After all, that's what I had always heard about gays while growing up in the '90s. For that matter, I still hear it today.

So, our friendship, and our trouble-making, continued. We followed the old familiar pattern: cause shit, get into shit, rinse, repeat. Then, about two years after our experiment with oral sex, we had another interesting sleepover, but this time, we actually stayed inside, which meant the neighbourhood's property was safe for a night. This time, Noah and I were joined by a friend of Noah's - Grayson. Grayson was older than both of us: he was two years my senior, and it was no secret that he was, for the most part, done with puberty. Meanwhile, Noah and I were in mid-pubescence, still fighting the good fight.

On this night, we talked and lounged around in different parts of the room, which was huge, probably thirty feet by twenty feet. It grew late, but we were still wide awake at 3 am. Grayson mentioned that he was bored, and not very tired, and someone suggested that, maybe if we masturbate together, like a circle jerk, we would fall asleep soon after, just like most dudes do after they cum. With the lights off, and only a single street light shining through the large double window, it was just bright enough to see each other's cocks and faces. All three of us took our cocks out slowly, and, with a hesitation born of embarrassment, we started to stroke them slowly, like "straight" buddies, just trying to get off. It was hard not to peek over at Grayson - he was older and more developed than most guys I had seen. All I could make out through my squinted eyes was at least six inches of erect thick penis, with lots of dark, bushy, pubic hair. This was an extreme turn-on for me, but I had no choice except to avoid letting him know how he was affecting me. It didn't take long until the awkwardness had us all finishing quickly. Silence followed, and the next morning, when we went out to roam the town, there was only "regular" conversation. Nothing was ever said about what we did that night.

Just before becoming a teenager, I had a few sexual encounters with schoolmates. With the boys, things happened outside, which is perhaps why I have never been a fan of sex outdoors. Still trying to figure it all out, I also had a few short-term girlfriends around this age. The memories of touching just the outside of a "girlfriend's" vagina didn't cause confusion, so much as it raised the question, "Do I like this nearly as much as I like being with boys?" This was also around the time our sexual education teacher's response to a student's question made me think to myself, "Oh, okay! This is just a normal part of puberty.

The kid responsible for this revelation was a typical trouble maker, and when our sex ed teacher asked if anyone had any questions, his words perked up my ginger head. He asked, "What if a guy likes another boy?" She replied, "It's normal for boys or girls to find something attractive in someone of the same sex. You may like another guy's hair or arms, and this is just a normal human reaction. There is nothing wrong with that." So, that meant, all of my attraction to boys was simply a part of puberty, and would eventually fade away, just like acne. Armed with this information, I felt a bit better about what I was feeling, since it was going to go away, and I would be "normal."

Now, my last childhood sexual experience with a guy happened when I was thirteen years old, and it's one that I will never forget. His name was Lucas, and this experience has stayed with me, I think, because he was basically a full-grown man. I had always been attracted to his type, so this was a big turn-on. Lucas was six-foot-four; he had a darkly tanned complexion, and shaggy, dirty blond hair. His body was covered in thick, dark, body hair, with a very dark scruff on his chiseled, square jaw and cheeks. His eyes were hazel, and his build was long and lanky. Lucas was a handsome guy, in a geeky kind of way, and in my book, at that age, he was a "man". I was thirteen years old when Lucas, who was a friend of the family, came to stay with us for about a month. He was just shy of his eighteenth birthday, but he could have passed for someone in his twenties.

Yes, he was handsome for sure; yet he exuded an insecure, desperate, horny teenage vibe. Lucas was incredibly friendly, but he was always desperate for the attention of girls. He talked a lot about getting pussy, making himself out to be a "player." This was SO not true. It was a classic case of telling stories, made up in order to come off as a highly sought-after "fuck boy." Lucas had a girl over once during his stay with us. He tried to make out with her in almost every room of the house. At one point he had her helping him make noises, as though they were fucking on the washing machine. Everyone in the house knew that it wasn't real. He was striking out, and after that, he never saw the girl again that I knew of. Jealousy, on my part, I admit, was tremendous.

I always wondered what it would be like to see the mature member between his legs. Sadly, all I would ever get to see was Lucas with girls who didn't appear to be interested in him. Never having a chance myself, I instead had to sit and witness his failures, and see the frustration on his cute, scruffy face. Lucas was mostly a homebody, and never really went out much, other than to go to work as a supermarket stock clerk in a local grocery store. One late evening Lucas and I were the only ones home. We decided to hang out in the living room and watch TV on our wood-framed, old-school floor model coloured television. Lucas and I were making small talk as we watched the recap of a baseball game from earlier in the day. Sports wasn't an interest of mine, but with just Lucas and me there, I thought, what better way to get his attention. So I went along with it, and pretended that I had as much interest in it as he did.

We were sitting on my family's very outdated flamingo pink L-shaped sectional couch - Lucas on one section of the sofa, me on the other. I had seen Lucas sitting before, obviously, but that evening he was sitting in a position I found a bit odd. Wearing shorts and a T-shirt, he sat with his legs spread, knees bent up in front of him, almost touching his chest, with his feet on the couch. Sneakily looking over, I could see his huge, hairy, manly testicles hanging out of his shorts. They were so large and hairy, just lying there, begging to be licked and sucked. I was silent for some time, thinking if I spoke, he would tuck the boys away again, and my thirteen-year-old spank- bank material would go away.

Watching him out of the corner of my eye, I could see Lucas scratching his junk, and still he left the boys out, which was starting to seem like it was being done on purpose. Snickering at the fact that they were still out and he didn't seem to care, he looked over and said to me, "What's so funny?" When I replied, "Nothing" he proceeded to bug me until I told him what I found so amusing. Nervous over what he might say or do, I told him, my heart racing, "Well, you're scratching your balls, and they're hanging out of your shorts." He looked down and just shrugged and put his legs down with his feet on the floor. This now afforded me a view of the complete outline of his semi-hard cock.

When a commercial came on the TV, Lucas looked over at me with a look on his face that said he was up to no good. "Hey, wanna go hang out upstairs and listen to music in my room?" I, of course, said yes, because I could tell he had something else on his mind, and I didn't want to miss whatever it might be. This could be my once-in-a-lifetime chance with a guy I had always crushed on. Lucas shut the TV off, and we went up to the bedroom. The first thing we did was play around with the radio until we could find some good music to listen to.

After settling on a station, we lay on the queen-sized water bed making small talk, with the music extremely loud. It was so loud that, at one point, I remember saying maybe we should turn it down in case someone came home. That way, we would be able to hear them come in. Lucas agreed, and once it was turned down, he stopped, looked me dead in the eyes, and said, "Now what?" I replied "I don't know, now what?" I laughed it off, even though my teenage-self was so highly nervous, I was surprised I didn't leave a sweaty outline of my body on the bed.

Lucas lay there with his legs spread open on the bed, and I could see the outline of his large throbbing cock. It was very close to eight inches in length, relatively thick, and uncircumcised, judging from the outline in his shorts.

It was a very awkward moment - we just lay there staring at each other. Soon, I found myself focusing on his shorts. Seeing his throbbing shaft, I gazed at it as if I was waiting for a flower to bloom. All I could imagine was ripping those shorts off and taking his large rock-hard cock in my mouth, showing him that I could be better than any of those girls he went out with. We shuffled around in the bed, the sexual tension mounting, and all I could think about were his hairy nuts and his raging rod now only six inches away from me. If his shorts had opened, his massive cock would probably have slapped me with great force, he was so hard, and I was so near. Oh, how I would have welcomed that!

There was so much tension in the air, I can't even explain how bad it was. Looking down at his shorts, there was a wet spot of what I could only assume was his salty pre-cum starting to pool. It was all I could do to not shove my face down in his crotch and start cleaning and finishing him off. My mouth was salivating, wanting to know what he tasted like. Still, I held back in case I was reading the signs wrong, but how can you misread lying in bed with someone who has a hard cock for over an hour?

This interlude of intensely doing nothing went on for a good hour and a half, with neither Lucas nor I making the first move. Highly frustrated, he got up, his fat cock holding up his shorts like a tent. I made sure he knew I noticed, but Lucas just looked at me, shrugged it off, and walked out of the room. Nothing happened between us that night nor any other night, but I'm certain he went into the washroom and blew his load hard within minutes of leaving the bedroom. Looking back, I regret not having made a move. I don't know if it's only so I could have had a better ending to a very hot moment in my early teens, or if I just wanted to conquer that big cock of his.

We never had a moment like that again, and two weeks later, he was on his way back home. I've only seen him once since then; I caught sight of him in public, with whom I assume to be his wife and three young kids. Lucas didn't look at all happy. When he noticed me, he walked the other way without even the slightest acknowledgment. Lucas was on my social media until I came out, and a short time after that, he removed himself. He is likely one of the many married men on hookup apps, looking for men to give them head or ass. Oh well, I missed my shot! But then again, he was hung, and I was young, so maybe I wouldn't have been able to take his gun.

When I was fourteen years old, I had a falling-out with my mother, Katherine, so I moved out, and into a friend's home with her and her family. My mother tried to get me to come home, even calling the police, but due to my age and having a safe roof over my head, there was nothing that could be done. Little did anyone know I was in a relationship with "my friend," who was thirteen years my senior. The age gap brought with it many issues and hardships, not to mention everything else added to the mix. Naturally, I was young and thought I knew everything about life, but the crazy thing was I had yet to recognize my own sexuality. I still thought I was going to get through puberty and my lust for men would be gone.

Even after my first child was born when I was sixteen - my "curiosity" continued to grow. Still thinking I was "normal," I found myself renting bisexual pornography, pretending when I got home that I didn't know what it was until it was already playing for my girlfriend and me. When scenes with two men came on, I would feign shock and confusion as to why there were multiple cocks with one woman in the scene. This way, I could try to determine whether or not my interest in men was just a passing phase of puberty, while at the same time, keeping my secret safe.

At the local privately-owned video store, I was able to rent bisexual porn because the owners didn't know my age, and the membership was in my girlfriend's name. One day, I returned an overdue video after the store owners had called for it a few times. When I arrived at the store, one of the owners was there, upset that I was returning it so late. My late fees were paid, and just as I was ready to walk out the door, she turned and looked at me and exclaimed, "I know what you are!" Mortified, thinking immediately, she knew I was gay, my mind raced. "OMG! How does she know? Do other people know? Is it because she's a lesbian and she has what people call, 'Gaydar'?

With the answers to those questions unanswered, I never returned to that video store. I felt it was best to be careful until I knew who I indeed was. People couldn't find out that I find men attractive, so I just tried even harder to hide it until I discovered my truth. The last thing I wanted was more shame than I already felt towards myself, and I didn't want my girlfriend and child to go through any pain because of my actions. These feelings were excruciating, and I was torn with confusion about my sexuality.

Other than seeing penises of friends when fooling around during my youth, I had never seen an adult man's erect penis except my own. When I watched those porn videos, I would see sculpted men kissing and touching one another; it made me feel guilty for being aroused by it. The guilt started to make me hate myself more, because these feelings towards men were not going away. My weight started to balloon, and I gained at least 80 pounds in less than a year, all from being ashamed because "a real man shouldn't be feeling this way towards other men." I saw myself as a freak. I was scared; what would people say about me if I was gay? I just wanted to be "normal" and not have any sexual attraction to men.

The mother of my children - I did love her for who she was. We had a bond, and this bond was largely built on our children. Our children, who melted my heart anytime I looked at or thought about them, just the same as today. Torn, I continued to tell myself that all these feelings were normal and part of maturing and that I wasn't gay or bisexual. I was "straight" - just going through puberty and growing up. This was all normal. Right?

BEHIND THE PICKET FENCE

. . . .

CHAPTER 6

"If your whole heart isn't in it, you shouldn't get married"

C onnie and I were lying in bed together in her sister and brother-in-law's home on a late summer's night in 1997. Connie, her family, and I were temporarily staying there. Connie and her family had been evicted from their home, and I was still living with them. I had a home and mother that I could return to, but I was only fifteen years old, and I was trying to prove something; to whom, I don't know. Anyway, Connie and I were just lying in the small, cluttered room, staring out of the open window, when we started talking about the future. Our conversation included what we both wanted in life family-wise, including kids and marriage. We discussed where we wanted to see ourselves in ten years, how many kids we saw in our future and our thoughts on marriage. The flood of ideas and questions had my head in a tailspin. I had never had to think about those things before as a very young teenager.

Fuck! These are questions that you usually don't think about all at once; you ponder them separately and slowly, over many years. There I lay, just a teenager who was confused about who he was and didn't have a clue what he wanted when it came to those big, adult life decisions. Still, I closed my eyes and let my mind get lost in thought and wonder. What did I want? My mind, generating thoughts and dreams of happiness, only took minutes to conjure an image. It was as if the results were being compiled by a search engine on the internet. With my eyes closed, I could see myself standing in the small eat-in kitchen of a quaint, well-kept home, with a child in front of me.

The child I envisioned in front of me was a boy, and from what I saw in my head, I was raising him alone. Fifteen years old, and this is what I imagined as my "White-Picket – Fence" life. But as of yet I had zero life experiences to go on to truly know what I wanted. Sometimes we jump into things without fully thinking them through just because they seem right at that moment. I don't know if what I was imagining as my future was true or just a spur-of-the-moment thought from being put on the spot. However, when I told Connie what I was envisioning in my mind, I remember leaving out the part about seeing myself raising the child alone. I was already confused and didn't know what I truly wanted: plus, men don't raise kids alone in any fairytales I had ever read or seen as a kid. Soon after the conversation ended, Connie and I had sex. This was when we started to dabble in not being as cautious as possible to prevent pregnancy.

Even at that young age, my mind couldn't create a future with a female in my head, although I could imagine a future with a kid (or kids). Not too long after that night, my desire to have a family with the perfect storybook ending was something that I started to crave. To have that life, I couldn't be gay, so I was pretty insistent at this point that it was my body just going through the waves of puberty and teenage hormones. I was straight! When thoughts of people having children and a family went through my head, I imagined them as being the picture-perfect "Hallmark" family. Perhaps I was dreaming of something that I didn't have growing up, and it was my way of drowning it out. My idea of the perfect family was like a scene from the television show, "Leave it to Beaver." That show featured a family home that you lived in your whole childhood: a white picket fence, siblings, a stay-at-home mom who made you breakfast after calling you down from bed each morning, and the hard-working father who was always there and always had time for you. Crazy, I know! This is what I believed family life was like for others.

When thinking of what I wanted for my life, I didn't quite see all that. The difference was that I saw myself as a single, working father of one child. This was the picture that formed inside my head when questions of this nature came out of left field. However, I couldn't share the complete picture with Connie. After all, even twenty years ago, we were taught that boys grow up to become men. They marry women, have children and live a fairytale life. This was like a late-night "as seen on TV" promo that ran non-stop through my adolescent head.

How was I ever going to conform to that lifestyle when I couldn't stop myself from staring at all the men around me? It wasn't like I was admiring what they were wearing. It was hardcore checking them out from head to toe and back again. Of course, I did this as clandestinely as possible to avoid detection. My mind was focused on the one thing I wanted to see - the adult male body in its full glory. My imagination ran wild, envisioning the dads, husbands, boyfriends or male partners behind all of these "White Picket Fences." This rampant curiosity forced me to find ways to contain my drool and stares - again, covertly - at the guys in my high school, especially in the changing room. The changing room fed my addiction at that point in my life: the aromatic muskiness of guys and their pheromones was too much to handle at times. Even the simplest things, like a classmate who was well-dressed and smelled great, made it hard not to need a book to block the view of the automatic pop-up tent in my pants.

Looking back, it's apparent that I was gay. Perhaps my confusion would have been lessened if there had been more open dialogue back then about same-sex attraction.

Maybe I would have believed acceptance was possible, regardless of my orientation. That's still a pipe-dream in many parts of the world today, and here I was hoping for it over twenty-plus years ago. If I had been taught these life-lessons at that crucial point in my young life, my story would be completely different from what it is today. In my experience, the worst thing someone can do when they believe a friend or loved one is gay or struggling to come to terms with their sexuality is to mock them or call them names. Even if people think that they're only "joking" about someone's sexuality, it's never right and it only causes humiliation and harm.

This is something that I struggled with a lot in school. Many times I was called "Gay" or "F*g" by classmates who thought they were being "cool" in front of their friends. In a way, I was lucky. Such bullying often leads to years of keeping one's sexuality hidden, or even commiting suicide. For me, the torture continued until I started having my kids; but even then, some people still thought this behavior was funny. They would typically say little things, such as "You're so gay!" While not overtly derogatory, it caused me to push back and keep myself from being open. My reply would always be the same "No, I am straight! Thanks!". After years of this form of bullying, paired with my confusion, I felt I had to prove that I was "straight" even if I wasn't.

As I started to live my "straight" life, my weight began climbing fast. It seemed being sexually active with a female was causing my weight to go up and down like a sex worker on a Friday night. Naturally, like many people in the world, I desired to have an ideal body that was lean and fit. Besides, societal standards taught me that possessing slim, firm, and chiselled features was absolutely essential for sexually attracting another person. So, if I were to transform myself into a model physical specimen, I would instantly find love and affection from someone. How stupid was I? But it's how the perfect fairytale goes, right? No one ever gets swept off their feet by a plump Prince Charming. Anyway, suppose I did find a way to drop the excess pounds? How was I going to iron out the wrinkles left behind from years of stress and weight loss? How could I rid myself of the thick, purple stretch marks on skin that once held hundreds of pounds of fat from stress eating? How would I change my hair color or facial hair growth? Should I (or could I) make my cock bigger, thicker or maybe more appealing? Oh, my gayness!

All these things in my head caused me to eat even more just to feel some semblance of comfort and security. Even though I knew these changes couldn't realistically take place without resorting to drastic measures, I still held onto the hope that it would happen someday, somehow. My problem was that I never just stopped to appreciate myself for who I was and what I had to offer as a person. I could only see what I thought was lacking. I couldn't get it in my head that I was more than all the superficial things I thought were required for gaining love and acceptance in my life. A porn star body, a pop-can-sized cock and a straight relationship were all I needed to have the "White Picket Fence" life. I had it all wrong, but no one was letting me in on the joke.

A few years into trying to live the perfect life, and struggling to be happy inside my own skin, I found myself continuing to gain weight, for reasons I couldn't understand at the time. I had, and still have, such a strong love for my family; from the outside, we looked like the perfect family.   But my head was sometimes so foggy, I felt like an outsider looking into someone else's life. Between the confusion about my sexuality, the pressures of day-to-day life, and the stress over finances upon my shoulders, the fogginess came more and more frequently. The possibility that I could still be genuinely attracted to the "wrong" gender, even after having my children, made me feel like a worthless waste of a man and a failure. My life was seemingly good when you glanced at it, from the outside, at a distance. However, there was pain deep inside that I unknowingly suppressed, and tried to smother it with food - the unacknowledged reality was, I just wanted dick.

Dick-desire and the method of comforting myself caused me much-added bodyweight. My silhouette was making me look like I was the one pregnant in the relationship. Food was my crack cocaine, and it helped me cope with issues I didn't know I had. In a way, food was a replacement for therapy, as it is to many. Anyway, when I looked at myself being a dad and husband, there was no longer a need to worry about my weight or looks.

Why would they matter anymore? It's not like I needed to attract anyone, plus if I didn't attract the attention of guys, hopefully, I wouldn't attract theirs when shyly sneaking stares at the ones I found attractive. Drawing any kind of attention to myself could have caused people to question my sexuality, which I knew I couldn't handle. I was STILL unsure. Taking time to explore my sexuality would consume my attention when I needed to be focused on my wife and kids, or so it seemed. Keeping my boat steady, and not rocking it, was my way to keep the focus off of me; hence I remained hidden for some time. If I was going to come to terms with my sexuality, I would have to delicately map out a coming-out plan to my wife and kids. On top of my already-monumental fears, was the knowledge that, if I ever were ready to come out, I would need to begin working on my crinkles, wrinkles and flaws. If I didn't work on those, I could count myself out of the dating pool when the time finally came. This may sound absurd, but it's the harsh reality of dating, not only for myself, but for most single people out there in the dating world.

In my experience, when you first meet a gay man, for a date, and he says things you want to hear, such as, "I want a man who is kind, caring, gentle, and romantic; someone I can grow old with," or anything close to this, it is, for the most part, bullshit. Usually, the opposite is true. The words are to get what they want as quickly as they can, just like curb-side pickup, quick and easy. It seems like most gay men only want a partner if they meet some extensive criteria. If you complete everything on the checklist, you may make it to a second interview. You must be kind, have a perfect body that is fit with extremely little extra body fat. Your cock must meet specifics, or your ass must take a pounding like a cheap piece of meat. His "cock specifics" will include length, girth, shape, circumcised or uncircumcised, pubic hair that is shaved, groomed or full bush: sometimes they also have genital piercing preferences on top of that.

The hardest thing for me that some require is for you to be specifically a top or bottom. This doesn't matter if you're incredibly compatible in all other areas and meet all the other prerequisites for them. If they have a 100% top or bottom preference, all else goes out the window if your position is not what they want. It's also my experience that you usually don't have to worry about your own sexual satisfaction, because it doesn't matter. The good majority only worry about themselves. You might also have to meet their financial requirements and their standard of living. Something that is also becoming extremely popular is the "open relationship," many enjoy having this kind of arrangement. These are just a few things that many will want and require. Make sure you know what you're worth and what you want before you entertain joining the dating scene. It may sound like bullshit to some, but these are my experiences, and the experiences of people I know. Let me tell you - for me, it's nowhere near bullshit, and I'm sure it's not just a "Canadian" thing, like igloos, maple syrup candies and ketchup chips.

Some readers may not agree with my observations, and may say with an eye roll, "That's not true," and to that I reply, "really? (insert my own eye roll)." The issue is that people don't want to admit that they genuinely have expectations or requirements; some don't even realize they possess them. Hell, I've probably been guilty of wanting or expecting some of these things at specific points in my life. Guilty as charged! If I did, I own it, and it was never my intention to cause harm. If I ever made someone feel as though they were not enough, I am genuinely sorry!

My life experience has shown me that men lie to get what they want. All the work they put in and the stories they devise, just so that they can squirt their salty load on your face or in your ass is incredible. It becomes so tiring, you can't help but wonder, "Why bother trusting anymore?" I might as well shoot a load in my own hand and slap it across my face. Doing it myself could be just the same, if not better - I wouldn't have to deal with the mental anguish or change my sheets after. Long story short: building a genuine mental and emotional connection with another man is difficult. It takes time, patience, and some give and take. If your needs aren't being met, why allow yourself to be used just for their sexual gratification?

Gay dating standards are ridiculous, but we have allowed them to develop over the years as apps and dating sites have become our new singles bar. Superficialness and being materialistic are at the top of the list in the dating and hookup world. Some men on these apps don't even meet their own standards, but they expect us to. We all have things we look for in a partner, but are they realistic? I have reached a point in my life where I have "requirements", such as taking care of oneself physically and financially. It doesn't mean that I am looking for someone with washboard abs, under two hundred pounds, with pure muscle and a large bank account. For me, it's just the need for my partner to respect himself enough not to eat burgers and fries seven days a week, and for him to be able to pay his bills. It's the simple things, no?

There are things that I prefer in someone for reasons of physical attraction, and that's only natural. We find some characteristics or features more beautiful than others. Does this mean that I couldn't fall head over heels for someone opposite? No, it doesn't! It's just a guideline for what I know will fit well with my personality. If I'm happy with myself and love myself, this is what matters, and whoever may come my way and I fall in love with, so be it. The most important thing is love for yourself. Your "Picket Fence" is whatever color you make it, whatever design you want, and whomever you wish to have behind it with you.

All too often, people try to exude the best life to make others envious. When I observe people doing this, it is hard not to laugh and shake my head. Inside I want to scream out, "Hey lady, put your seemingly perfect life back in your purse! I've seen your husband cruising for dick". I've had to learn to face the blatant truth: we live in a world of sex, lies and cheaters. This goes for both men and women, no matter what their sexuality may be. Time and time again, people stay in relationships, even though behind closed doors it is a toxic situation. The perfect facade may be a show for jobs, family, or any number of reasons. With the temptation of easily accessible sex from apps on our electronic devices, it's hard to believe that anyone can be faithful to another person. My mind tells me, if I have always been faithful, there must be others like me that exist. Right? If that's the case, why are they so hard to find? I crave a connection, which makes having meaningless sex with someone difficult. Yes, I have done it, just as the majority has.

For me, though, it was mainly due to loneliness. No innocence here; I've taken part in threesomes with men, including men who are in open relationships, and only "play" together. When I have taken part in a couple's open relationship, I couldn't help but wonder why they would do that if they're in a genuinely loving partnership. Possibly this is me being a prude, since I have joined them in their bedroom, and now, here I am, questioning and judging their life decisions? As the saying goes, "Each to their own!"

For some couples, maybe this is a perfect arrangement. It spices things up in the bedroom and keeps one partner from potentially cheating on the other. Are these things that you now have to do to keep the relationship together? What would happen if you said to your partner, with whom you have an open relationship, that you no longer want to allow others to join in? Would they wander, cheat or even leave? It seems as though love and loyalty disappear when couples open up their relationships for sexual pleasure. Once the relationship is in an open state, there is a sudden abundance of jealousy.

Does my original vision of the "White Picket Fence" even exist anymore? If so, I have never seen it within my own family, before or after coming out. My "White Picket Fence" life has consisted of me hiding my sexuality, living penny to penny and just scraping by daily, being evicted, and moving from place to place, supporting a spouse who worked maybe ten percent of the time we were together, and having to request the help of food banks so that I could feed my family. Like I said, my kid's mother worked about ten percent of the time when we were together, and it was never full-time. Maybe a stay-at-home spouse was once part of the "White Picket Fence" life that I have envisioned, but not like this. I was working for the vast majority of the time my kids were growing up, and when I wasn't working, I was in school to further my education. Sometimes I would have to be in school full-time while working to support my family. I have children and a home that I don't own, so if it counts, maybe I could say I've had a piece of the "White Picket Fence." If there is this magical life, and it does exist, I truly believe it is a rarity, and the people who do have it need to cherish and nurture it.

All too often, humans try to live a "White Picket Fence" life. In my experience, for most, it's just a front or, at best, the honeymoon phase of a relationship. The number of married people secretly playing around on dating sites or apps is astounding. On gay apps, you see many married men giving specific times that their spouse or partner is at work, so you can "conveniently" come over and hookup. It's scary for me to even think of it, and I was a married man. When I was married, I never hooked up with other men or cheated on my wife, even after coming to terms with my sexuality. I did this out of respect and common decency, so my decisions wouldn't potentially affect her health. Many of the men I have seen on these sites request bareback (unprotected) sex daily from different men.

How can you do any of that and go home to your wife and kids? Entirely mind-blowing for me that, instead of growing balls and coming out to at least their spouse (as they already know their true sexuality), they cheat. A plethora of these same men are also the ones who scream their homophobic remarks at people, and later, they're bent over a tree in the park at night, taking another man's cock and load of cum up his ass. Big, nasty, bigoted asshole in front of friends and family: yet at the same time, he can blow cum bubbles out of his actual asshole. Excuse me, sir? I think your "White Picket Fence" has fallen!

LETTING GO

....

CHAPTER 7

*"Sometimes, the warmest thing to touch
your body is your tears."*

The worst thing I ever did in my life was to make excuses when I did something wrong, or to try getting out of doing something. Excuses did nothing positive for me, and only delayed my growth as a person. The way I live my life now is the way that I should have done from day one with Connie, when I was fourteen years old. If I had been open and honest, I would likely have experienced a very different start to my life as a young adult. Looking back on the life that I led back in the late 1990s, I wish it could have been like today; open and honest, with no bullshit. Life experiences as a parent, and lessons learned from being deceived by the men who have come and gone in my life have caused my filters (and blinders) to fall by the wayside. I no longer feel the need to be a bakery, and sugarcoat anything: the only thing that needs to be

118

sweetened before being swallowed is bullshit. If you're honest, there is nothing to worry about. Maybe if I had been straightforward with Connie early on, and advised her of my attraction to men, we would have had a different outcome. Perhaps we would have been one of those couples who has an open relationship for a short period, until mutual hatred grows to the point of divorce, due to jealousy.

Pain in life is inevitable; however, I wish I would have been able to take away the pain that I caused Connie and my kids, while also finding it possible to truly be happy. It's still hard to let go of all that happened - letting go is like trying to take a breath underwater. No matter how much I need to and want to, I just can't. I can't let go of the guilt I feel for the pain I may have caused my children as a parent. Holding on to the past won't change the outcome. My brain knows this, but my heart refuses to listen. Still, no matter how other people live their lives or tell you how to live yours, there is no excuse for not moving forward. It has been over ten years, and I still struggle with this.

My pain flows like a river of tears streaming from my eyes regularly. On top of the pain, there are moments of extreme loneliness that hit hard, like a brick thrown at my face. Being alone in this world can be scary; fears of not loving or being loved can only be kept buried for so long. When the lonesomeness hits, sometimes, the warmest thing to touch your body is your tears. People will say things like, "It's no one's business what happens behind closed doors." They're right, but I can tell you, what people think happens behind those doors is not accurate for the most part. For instance, behind my doors, I spend a lot of time sitting and pondering what I could change about my life; I cry, and then cry some more. People seem to believe that those who don't identify as straight must all be living a life of promiscuity, with a revolving door to the bedroom.

We are all human, and we all go through many emotions in life, no matter the sexual orientation. Half of me knows what I need to do in order to live a healthy life, mentally and physically. However, the other half still blames myself for not maintaining a "straight" lifestyle, and throwing that curveball at my family. Every day, it feels like I'm running from the police, because I have done something wrong, yet the only thing that I'm running from is my own happiness. These conflicting emotions cause many other negative thoughts to run through my head. Why be afraid just to be me? Why can't I live without these feelings of guilt and regret? I came out to live my life, but most of the time I find myself lurking in the shadows, wondering what it would be like to take the plunge and go wild, like so many other gay men. Maybe if I just let go, I could find peace within myself. Perhaps if I didn't worry so much about imagined life-altering consequences, I could let myself be free.

Freedom without fear would be like opening my phone, selecting the app of my choice, connecting with a guy offering NSA (No Strings Attached) sex, and just letting it happen. Give this random man my address, now to wait and see what comes next.

Within thirty minutes, a text comes in: "I'm here" to which I reply, "Be right there." I go down to the door and welcome this man from the app (whose name I didn't bother to ask) into my house, and we head to the bedroom. No words except "Hello's" are exchanged. Clothes are quickly ripped off, and he drops to his knees, taking my cock in his warm, slippery mouth, sucking like he is going to be late for Sunday dinner at grandma's house. I pull him up with a slight tug on his medium-dark blond hair. We begin kissing, and I can taste my cock on his lips and smell it on his breath. This was now turning me on wildly, so I throw him down on my bed. I take his average and respectable six-inch cock in my mouth and suck so hard and fierce that his back arches with each moan.

Within minutes I put his legs up in the air, asking him to hold them in place. As he grabs the back of his thick hairy legs, my face dives down to his puckered hole. The musky scent of his sweaty untrimmed hole arouses me so greatly that my cock begins dripping with pre-cum over the side onto the bedding. My face is now at his hole, like a dog on a piece of raw meat. Drilling my tongue deep inside his asshole, he yells, "HOLY FUCK!". To his surprise, I let up on his clean wet hole and climb on top of him. I grab his wrist while holding him down, and we begin to make out harder than teenagers under the stairwell in high school.

Now I'm subjecting him to tasting his sweet hole on my lips. As our make-out session continues, I gyrate my hips, teasing his cock by rubbing his pre-cummed tip all over my smooth tight hole. His musk drives me wild, so much so that I move quickly from his lips and begin to suckle on his nipples. His chest is carpeted in thick dark hair, and only heightening my horniness. My ability to control myself from going down on his cock is gone, so naturally, I begin giving it an excellent deep throat, cleaning his leakage. This doesn't last long, as his thick pubic hair in my face takes me over the edge of horny. I immediately move back up to kiss him; this time, as we kiss, I grab and slide his six inches of throbbing thunder into my tunnel of darkness.

He begins to thrust and hammer his cock deep within me, not even giving me a second to enjoy the ride. I'm so turned on at this point, and his thrusting in and out lasts for less than a minute before he exclaims he's going cum. His body tenses, and there's intermittent moaning, telling me he's now cumming inside of me. Knowing it's ending, I stay on him and continue to ride him as I jerk my cock quickly because he wants me to get off of him so he can leave. I blow my load all over his carpet of hair before the ride ends. I hand him a towel to clean himself off before dressing. Once dressed, he exclaims, "That was great, thanks!" And within seconds, he's gone, never to be heard from again.

That was a genuinely imaginary mix of how my experiences have gone and would probably have continued if I let myself live without fear of judgment and consequences. The truth is, the majority of hookups are usually very short-lived. The fictional experience above, had it actually happened, would have lasted a total of approximately fifteen minutes, and would have most likely ended in disappointment. It has been my choice not to fully let myself go; to not be careless and free. There have been a few times when I allowed myself to be irresponsible, but that always came with the aftermath of guilt and disappointment. One of those times was shortly after I came out. Connie and I were living in separate apartments, and man; I was feeling good and alive. I had never been able to let loose before, and the urge to do some of the things I had never fathomed I would ever get the opportunity to try was overpowering, and I sure grabbed my chance.

It was Pride 2011, held in Toronto, Ontario, and I was there! I'm sure the mass amounts of alcohol I consumed contributed dramatically to my bad choices that weekend; a weekend of absolutely poor decisions and fun memories. But would I do it all again? Most likely not! That weekend included fucking around with a guy I had met online weeks before, and we had been talking on the phone right up until Pride weekend. He lived an hour north of Toronto, and I lived an hour south of the city, so we had never met in person. We decided to meet for the first time at Pride. It was disappointing face-to-face. He was not what I was expecting: I have never been turned on by a younger Mr. Bean look-alike. Bean Jr. took over an hour to come down from his hotel to meet my friends and me on the street - he wouldn't tell me which one he was staying in. These should have all been signs to run and run fast, but hell, it was Pride! I figured he was a sure thing, and I knew a fair amount about him (I thought) from our conversations on the phone. Anyway, when he finally arrived, you could see in his face that Bean Jr. was planning on ditching me, but he soon changed his mind. These are some of the highlights of the short time we had together during Pride:

- I was caught giving Bean Jr. a blow job on the counter of a hotel lobby bathroom, as an older man walked in on us. He was not impressed, and we had to leave with exceptional speed (and business left unfinished) before security was called.

- We had been drinking most of the night, on top of what I had already downed while day drinking. We stopped and decided it was an excellent idea to make out on a street corner while waiting for the street light to turn green. Once the light changed, we proceeded to cross the street, when a Black BMW with four men pulled up and stopped us. They asked what we were doing, and Bean Jr. and I just looked at each other in confusion. We looked back at them, and without saying anything, the guy in the passenger seat went to pull and point a gun at us. It was to our luck that a police car was coming up behind them, and as they were stopped in a no-stopping zone, they had no real option but to move along. At that moment, it became clear how much hate is still out there in the world. If we had been male and female kissing, the chance of that happening would have been slim to none.

- Even after that scare, we still proceeded to make other poor decisions. We stumbled our way to a dark alley at 3a.m. The alley was close to the vehicle my friends and I were sleeping in for the night: our hotel room had been given away before we arrived for check-in. In the dark, I finished what I had started in the hotel lobby washroom. Kneeling on black metal stairs in an alley is not as fun as it sounds. Please, take my word on it!

After our adventures, including some in and out of hotel rooms and bars, he left to go back to his hotel room with his friends, and I went to the vehicle for some sleep. The following day, my two female friends and I woke up bright and early with the sun shining, and the day's heat already present. One friend was so drunk the night before that she had vomited out of the vehicle window. Even better, she was also on her menstrual cycle, and in her drunken state, she removed and threw her used tampon right out of the vehicle window. It was hard not to laugh when the car parked next to us moved, and there was her dried, used, and shriveled up tampon just baking in the sun. Great times! Great laughs! I would never do it again.

After some of those great times, I often stare into the mirror and wonder, "What am I doing now? Who is it I am becoming? Will I ever be skinny or fit? Will I ever be attractive enough to find my Prince Charming? Will I ever meet the standards of so many in the community?" I know I must keep these thoughts at bay so I can rationalize with myself, "If he genuinely is Prince Charming; I am enough just the way I am." The problem is that things take time, and in a world of quick and convenient, I don't want to wait. If I need emotional support or a hug, I want it now. Is it selfish of me to like someone just for the emotional connection? We need intellectual stimulation and emotional support in our lives, not just physical/sexual compatibility. After the last decade, when I look at my personality, I find myself more demisexual than anything, regarding sexuality. Demisexual is someone who needs an emotional connection with someone before becoming involved with them. This may be one of the reasons I became involved with Connie. She and I had a great connection, and we could talk for hours on end in the beginning years.

When it comes to Connie and our relationship now, it may seem as if I am mad at her, and some people will say to me, "You must be so angry with her! " At a point in my life, there was a lot of anger, but no longer. Disappointment is what I feel towards her; disappointment because she didn't make the life we had easier. By easier, I don't mean that I wanted to drop all my responsibility and have her do it all. I'm talking about Connie failing to pull her own weight within our relationship and family. Most days, I had to be the responsible one. People on the outside may have thought they saw a devoted housewife taking care of our four beautiful children. This is very debatable! For example, after our first child was born, for the majority of the first year of my daughters' life, I was the only one to bathe her.

As we continued to have more children, her responsibilities had to change with the growing family, and that was when Connie had to start doing things she didn't want to. Her responsibilities were always performed at a bare minimum level; never above and beyond, ever! So, I guess you could say yes, what those people on the outside saw was partially true: she was home taking care of the children, but to what extent? Back then, I would either be working full-time, or be enrolled in school full-time, with full funding to support my family. In school, my program coordinator knew my circumstances, and I was offered a paid placement for my credit. At home, I was the one who took care of the bills, maybe poorly, but at least someone was doing it. Connie didn't drive, so I had to do all of the driving, including shopping for groceries and any other appointments or errands that had to be done. Even after a long day of school and working, I would return home, and have to make dinner, whether it was just for me, for Connie, or for everyone. The typical excuse was, "I didn't know what you would want, what to make, or you make it better than I do!"

Our house was never in even a semi-clean state unless we had family or friends coming over. I didn't clean much for many of those years, either. My mentality was, "I worked all day. Connie could at least clean a single room every few days." I always felt like I was expected to do everything, because she was a "full-time mom," at home with the kids all day. But Connie being home all day was not my choice; it was hers, because she found it too difficult to work and take care of the children. It was okay that I had to, but it was always different for her. Had Connie worked full-time like me, it would have been easier to get outside help for the kids, and we could have had a better life for ourselves and our children.

Stress always seemed to be piled on top of my shoulders miles high, and I did everything possible to be what I thought a husband should be. When my mother-in-law, Ruth's health worsened, she came to live with us for a short time, making seven bodies in our happy home. This was at a time when Connie was actually working part-time; an extreme rarity. (This was the same job that she later told me she despised, and she said she felt as though I "forced her" to work.) While Ruth lived with us, I was the one who cleaned her from top to bottom, took care of her, and kept her as comfortable as possible. This was extremely hard to do, and it ate away at me, as Ruth was a very nasty woman. She freely expressed her very hurtful opinions of me and of my relationship with her daughter. She would regularly say things with me in close earshot, like how she wished I would die, how she hoped I would be hit and killed by a transport truck, along with many other nasty things. I was never good enough, except when I was doing something for her or her family.

When I was fourteen and Connie 27, Connie's sister Karen, 25, who was even nastier than their mother, and her brother Kenny 23, all lived at home with their parents, and were collecting social assistance. In the home, there were seventeen cats, three dogs, and a few smaller animals as well. The home smelt like a barn and had animal shit, piss and puke on the floors. This should have been a warning sign of what living with Connie outside the home would be like. Kenny was the only one besides me doing extra work outside the home to bring in extra money for the family. Their parents were collecting their old-age pensions, and I had to work at a local campground. The money I earned was used towards groceries and cigarettes for Connie's parents and myself. While working at the campground, I often stole food items before leaving for the day. These were taken from the camp's snack shack freezer, where I worked, and I worked alone. I took these things to help feed Connie, her family and myself, and at the time, I felt that I was doing the right thing. I was never told any different. No one ever tried to explain that what I was doing was wrong.

Connie essentially stole parts of me that I can never get back. If she had only shared the responsibilities to take some of the burdens off of me, perhaps I would have been able to have focused more on living, and not just surviving. I did whatever I could to keep the stress down in our home. Hell, I even tried to make it easier by paying a cleaner to come in and clean our house once a week. This helped slightly, but it also brought new stress to the table because it was more money that we had to shell out. We couldn't afford it, but I couldn't live in the filth and Connie's hoard.

No matter what part of our relationship Connie and I were in, I was always the bad guy; from the start to the end of the relationship, and even to this day. My character was always bad-mouthed no matter what I did for Connie and her family. Even after we split, and were still civil and friends with one another, Connie continued to talk shit, and make up lies about me. So, it came to the point where I just had to throw my hands in the air, say enough is enough, and cut all ties with her.

This massive breaking point happened after she was evicted from her home again and had no place to move her or the children's belongings. This happened at the only time I moved out of town for work and didn't have the kids full-time. Since I had the kids 80% of the time before this move, I asked Connie if she wanted to move in and take over the lease of the home I lived in. She agreed to this, and I moved to Toronto, Ontario, for my job, but still saw and spoke with the kids as much as I could during the months that I was gone. My time living out of town lasted a total of eight months. During those eight months, I would bring groceries back during my visits, or if I wasn't going there on a day off, I would drive there and bring them back to my apartment for a visit, either altogether or one at a time. In addition, I ensured that she received the income from the   person who rented a room in the house, along with any government tax credits that I received for the kids. This money was not paid directly to Connie, but to the homeowner, to ensure it went to the right place.

Since the lease was still in my name, I continued paying the owner directly for a short time. Connie was responsible for paying less than $800 per month for the home and bills. Even this was a challenging task, as she was awful at managing her money, causing a tough time to collect the remaining money for the lease. When it reached the point where she was only paying me $200 most months, I decided that I couldn't keep the home in my name. After speaking with the owner, it was agreed between all three parties that Connie could have the lease transferred over in her name. Knowing she was a poor money manager, I hoped that this would be the turning point where she would "grow up" and start to make proper adult decisions. Shit in one hand, and wish in another!

While I was in Toronto and the time Connie had the home in her name, I found out that the power and gas supply to the house had been disconnected. It hurts me knowing what the kids had to go through because Connie wasn't adult enough to find and secure gainful employment to support them even fifty percent of the time. Fucking hell! She wasn't even adequately supervising them. Connie was their friend first and mom...well, maybe second. It kills me still inside that my children never got to experience true, actual parents. I made many mistakes as a young, confused, homosexual man who tried his hardest. Connie...well, I don't think I will add anymore of her faults and mistakes. She knows her truth, but she's too self-absorbed to ever speak of them truthfully. These issues tipped me over the edge and caused the end of our friendship. I just became too upset with her for allowing these things to happen. Never were there signs of Connie even trying to make a better life. It was as if she liked merely surviving and doing as little work as possible.

Once when I was picking up the children, I told her that I had lost all respect for her, and we have never spoken more than a few words at a time to each other since approximately 2014. After considering everything that was happening with the kids, I moved back in early 2015 and once again, they came to live with me full-time after I secured a home in the area. Once they moved back with me, they didn't even see their mother that year for

Christmas until days after the holiday: this was Connie's decision. The four children, a home, bills, and feeding everyone was not cheap, and I was doing it myself by just scraping by. So, I had to ask Connie for some support. Support for her children - for even just groceries - even once. She told me she couldn't afford it. Even though she was living with a friend and collecting government money for the kids that she didn't have in her care - she still said she could afford it.

When the kids finally had their Christmas visit with her that year, she sent them home with a gift for me. When I opened it, my blood began to boil. Her gift to me was a somewhat pricey box of chocolates, with a card addressed to me. Inside the card were hundreds of dollars in gift cards for different places. Yet when I asked for $100 to help feed her children, she declined it because she said she couldn't afford it.

She wasn't even seeing them at all; essentially, she was a "deadbeat" parent, and she decided to slap me across the face with gift cards for me, when she couldn't help feed her kids. That was the only time she gave me anything monetary during all the time I had the children full-time, and that wasn't even meant for them. But, I used those gift cards to feed the kids as any responsible parent would. Connie has never provided any support in any way, even though I have had the kids more than 80% of the time for close to a decade, except for the months I lived in Toronto for work. Connie came into some money in 2021, and she never offered even the smallest amount to try and make right for all those years. She has continued to do for herself only, and to try to buy the love of others with it.

Connie is a selfish, self-centered, middle-aged woman, to whom I lost my virginity and had children. It's hard not to feel that she stole a part of each kid's childhood, as well as a part of mine. To see selfishness, and to know that someone doesn't care enough about their actions to at least try and make things right, is heartbreaking. The money doesn't matter. A sincere apology would have been better than any amount of money, but that window of opportunity only stays open for so long. In the end, we just have to live with the guilt of our actions. I chose my initial path in life with Connie; my happiness and highlights are all from my kids. For that, I am incredibly grateful. Since the age of sixteen, there is nothing that I would not do for my kids, living penny to penny just to feed them and hold a roof over their heads. My kids may not have had the things in life that other children had, such as brand-name clothing, top electronics or vacations to Disneyland, but I did try my best. Now I need to try and let go of the things that cannot be changed.

LOVING
ANONYMOUSLY

. . . .

CHAPTER 8

*"I'll let you play with mine if I can
play with yours."*

My mind has always been boggled by the disrespect that some people have for their life partners. How can one be unfaithful, then return home to them afterwards, as if nothing is wrong, and still hold the love they have always had? Here is the question burning in my mind: "Is the love for their partner real if they feel the need to cheat?" I have expressed my thoughts on this, and people say things like, "People make mistakes in life. " Absolutely! However, this doesn't mean that the person will change their behavior. Essentially, they have just burned the bridge of trust and must try rebuilding it. The issue with that is, the partner will always wonder in the back of their mind if the other person is still cheating. Even when they say they trust you, they're still stressing that you're off fucking someone else. These experiences can cause life-long problems for the partners. Those who have been cheated on will bring that history to every future relationship.

No one wants to go through pain, so it's in our nature to protect ourselves from allowing it to happen again. It's unfortunate, because, in a new relationship, both parties should be able to give and expect complete trust from the start. Giving my trust to a man at the beginning is extremely difficult for me, after all the pain that I have gone through in the past, but I stop and think about what I want in a new relationship. How would I feel if I wasn't given the trust I deserve because of something that happened in their past? It would be like I was being punished for their ex's mistakes, which is unfair to any party involved.

Judging from my experiences in the gay community, monogamy and trust are not the norm; actually, they're extremely rare. No finger-pointing; I'm just as guilty of not giving trust, due to my negative experiences, as the next man. Even before coming out, I was aware that people can be unfaithful in a multitude of different ways, and that was always a concern. What I didn't realize was how many people would rather sneak around and do these types of things instead of just being open and honest about it. When I look back, I can't say that I was fully open and honest with Connie about everything when we were together; never was I unfaithful, but neither could I be open about how I was feeling inside sexually. I should have, and I know this now, because, had I been honest with her, she would have had the choice of staying or not. She would have had control over deciding what she could and could not handle.

I'm still judged for my choices in the way I came out and for waiting so long. Strangers say things like, "So, you left your family to go fuck young, 'twinks,' buy drugs, and spend your children's college funds on the people you're dating." HA! Joke's on them - I was too poor to have college funds for my kids! But they have all made it with their education so far. This is the only part of my story that frustrates me so much. People who don't know my story, judge me harshly, based on their own inaccurate assumptions. They don't know my life.

The people I refer to are often the same ones who cheat behind their partner's back, but won't come forward and have a frank discussion about sexuality or other issues that they're having in the relationship. Making hard decisions and having those hard conversations are even more problematic when left for later down the road when the cheating is discovered, and yes, it will always be discovered. Worse still, the victim doesn't always tell the cheating partner right away that they know. The hurt and distrust is given time to fester. This is just my personal opinion, perhaps because I am and have always been a very monogamous person, and exes have always liked to try and stick their dicks in random holes behind my back.

Fuck, I swear some of these men were born with a "if they have a warm hole, stick it in" mentality. What one does with their body and life is their choice, and we all are a product of our life choices. But, if your choices could potentially harm the person you're with, it is no longer just about you. Maybe if you had an open conversation with your partner, you could find solutions to make both parties happy. Many gay couples choose to be in open relationships or marriages, and the number of couples choosing this lifestyle is growing extremely fast. This way of living, in my opinion, is something that both parties would have to fully agree on.

If you're in a relationship with completely open and honest communication, it leaves it to each person to make their own educated decision if they want to stay in the relationship or not. They then have the power to decide if the relationship is still suitable for them. It's a scary feeling to be so open with someone, but you don't know how the other party will react. You don't know if they will leave the relationship because the issues discussed are too much for them to handle. For this reason alone, people often lie, so they can still have the life they want, both at home and behind the scenes. This is utterly selfish and in no way gives your partner a say in what's best for them.

During a recent browse on a well-known gay hookup app, I crossed paths online with a person who exemplifies exactly what I am talking about. Maxwell, this guy I came across, had posted a generic, sparse profile. He sent me a message first, including a headshot photo. He asked me what I was looking for; after warning him that I don't enjoy hook-ups and that I like to get to know a person a bit first before even meeting, he agreed that it seemed an excellent way to start. So we asked each other questions back and forth, mainly general stuff like work, hobbies, likes and dislikes and so on. He sent more photos of himself, all fully clothed, which I have to say was a shock for this app. However, I couldn't help but notice something. To the left side of this one photo, there was a minimal amount of hair visible, indicating that there was another individual partially in the picture. Detective mode kicked in, and I figured it was either an ex or current partner, so I went back to his profile to see if his relationship status was listed. Of course, it wasn't.

That was all the information I needed to confirm that he was in a relationship and cheating on his partner. I mean, really - a limited profile, location settings turned off, no relationship status, and a cropped photo? My curiosity was piqued to see his reaction to my next question, so I asked without hesitation, "Are you single"? To my surprise, Maxwell replied honestly. He confessed that he was, in fact, in a long-term relationship, but his partner was coming to terms with being asexual. I decided to probe further, so I asked if his partner was aware that he was looking for sex elsewhere. Once again, Maxwell shocked me and was very honest. He said no, but also that his partner was not sexual at all with him. He stated that they have been sexual together maybe three times within a year. Curious, I asked if this, "anything sexual," included such things as jerking off together, jerking off each other, oral sex, eating one another's ass or anal sex, and he said yes, out of all of these things, a total of three times.

My mind was so fucking intrigued at this point I had no clue if what he was telling me was truthful or not. However, he wouldn't have any reason to lie to a perfect stranger to try and get sex. It would have been easier just to say he was single and leave it at that. Our conversation continued, and he explained to me that he had asked his partner about having an open relationship. His partner was totally against the idea. My mind was bursting with curiosity as to why the two of them were even in a relationship in the first place. At one point in the conversation, I mentioned that I always like to give an "outsider's" perspective on any given situation. He asked for my thoughts on the matter, so I put my two cents in. This is how my conversation with Maxwell went, from the message when I asked if he was single:

Me-So you're single?

Maxwell-No, actually, I'm not. My partner (of 6 years) is, I think, slowly coming to terms with his asexuality. We have so much love between us, but we've had sex maybe three times in the last year. People, of course, have needs, *which is why I'm here on this app. I don't want to make him feel bad about never having sex, but I also don't want to go never having it again. So this seems to be my only option.*

Me-*Wow! That is a bit of a stretch on the sex. So, I sympathize with your situation. Sometimes medications can make you basically not want sex at all, and when you do have sex, it takes a while to come to completion.*

Maxwell-*He's not on any meds at all. It's been difficult, to say the least. I've asked for an open relationship a few times, thinking that could work for him as well, but he was and still is very opposed to the idea. I would never leave him. So I'm unsure of what else I could do.*

Me-*So… does he know you're going elsewhere?*

Maxwell-*No he doesn't. That's why I'd prefer to find a FWB. I don't care much for just random hookups either, but sometimes I go for it just because it's been so long*

Me-*So he doesn't want to have sex but doesn't want to discuss how he can make it better for you? Does he know you have Grindr?*

Maxwell-*Correct! I think he's mostly feeling a lot of shame. He's never been one to talk much about how he's feeling anyway. And no, he doesn't.*

Me-Wow! Definitely, an interesting situation you're in. I don't know how I would handle it.

Maxwell-I could be doing this all wrong. Maybe I'm a bad person for being on here in secret, but I love him way too much to consider leaving.

Me-See, I am one who really thinks about the reasons behind people's behavior, not as a judgment, just more of my personal observation.

Maxwell-So...you have any thoughts or ideas?

Me-Sometimes, no matter how much you love someone or know someone, the love can cause blinders. We only see what we are willing to accept or can handle. When two people are together, and they have, for example, a mixed financial situation, such as a house that runs on both incomes ,etc., or when vehicles or house/apt are in both names, we tend to have a false sense of love. We get stuck in the situation of being comfortable and accepting of what we will tolerate. We think that they would never do anything to hurt or betray us, because they love us. Yet, sometimes they know so well how we function and how we think, that they use that knowledge to play us. It's easier for them to stay, because it's so comfortable, and they're getting what they want. Is that true love - for us or for the *person doing that to us? Many times people are unhappy with something in the relationship and don't want the threat of something happening to rock the boat so they become sneaky and use excuses to explain away why they're being a certain way,   like not having a desire for sex when it really is/could be they're getting fulfilled elsewhere, whether physically or virtually. To hide their lack of desire, they make excuses, and if they're good enough, their partner won't be any the wiser. Look at what you're doing (not judging). He doesn't know. Why is that? Because you have made sure to cover your tracks because you love him. Who's to say he is not doing the same thing? Again, we can love someone, but that doesn't mean we are IN love with them. I have been there, and in the end, it wasn't until my mental health began to suffer that I sought help. After it was over, I found out that he had been doing things behind my back for months and months. Too often we don't pay enough attention, and don't realize our comfortable relationship is an illusion. Can you live your whole life fulfilling your sexual needs behind his back? Or do you think that perhaps it's time for a serious conversation with him? Sorry! Just an outsider's view, and a view from someone who has been in a similar situation.*

__Maxwell__-Okay! Totally see all the valid points you made. You're right in wondering if this is what I'd be willing to do for forever. Never thought about that. I should say that we've never been a couple that has had lots of sex. In 6 years, if we've had sex 20 times, I'd be surprised. So, I don't *think he's doing anything behind my back, but again how would I know, as you said. Maybe it's time for another conversation about it all.*

Me-*Every situation is different. Not saying what I wrote is what it is, just my opinion on it. Anal 20 times in 6 years? Or like blow jobs, hand jobs and anal in total?*

Maxwell-*Any type of sex, maybe 20 times. Maybe half that was anal sex.*

Me-*So if you don't mind my asking. In the first month of you guys seeing each other, how many times did you have any form of sex?*

Maxwell-*We didn't have any type of sex until almost a year in.*

Me-*And were you okay with it being that way? Or did you have conversations about it?*

Maxwell-*After about six months, I questioned it. He was my first real relationship, so that was a big part of it. He didn't want us to rush through anything.*

Me-*How soon after you started dating/talking did you move in together? P.S. Please tell me to shut the fuck up at any point. I won't take offense. The hardest questions in a* relationship are normally the ones we don't want to know the answers to.

Maxwell-It was about two years. I'd gotten a full-time job, and we were both fresh out of college.

Me-So in that time, neither one of you really questioned the sexual part of your relationship?

Maxwell-I had once. We had a real conversation about it. He told me he's never been overly interested in sex but still enjoys it every so often.

Me-Just because you have been together a long time, don't let your contentment keep you from making hard decisions. These decisions only become harder as time goes on.

Maxwell-Fair enough!

Me-Does he jerk off, or are there signs that he is jerking off behind your back? Does he care if you are jerking off?

Maxwell-We both jerk off frequently, both of us discreetly.

Me-*So does it not raise a red flag that he is enjoying getting off discreetly yet doesn't want sex? Sometimes we paint those red flags green to keep ourselves from rocking the boat. Why is it, "discreetly," and not enjoyed together?*

Maxwell-*Well IDK if discreetly is the right word. We have very opposite schedules also. He may jerk off maybe once every 2 or 3 weeks, whereas I'm like, every 2 or 3 days :)*

Me-*Understandable*

That is where the conversation stopped completely. He never messaged again until maybe four months or more later, when I received one from him. He didn't remember who I was at first: it was a new account for me. I had not been on there for a few months, so I had to re-download the app. Once I helped jog his memory, he remembered our conversation. He still tried again to get me to hook up with him, and this time he sent nude pictures of himself. My position stands, and I will not have sex with someone to help them cheat on their partner. He messages on and off, but the more he finds he is not getting what he wants, the fewer the messages come. His situation truly is sad, but open communication is really needed. If you need sex and your partner doesn't, you need to figure shit out between the both of you.

When looking at myself and others on dating apps and sites, it seems likely that many users have been damaged in one way or another. This is based on my experiences with men, but I'm sure it is just as prominent for females who use similar sites. We take to dating online for a variety of reasons, such as:

* It's easy to hop online and possibly meet or chat with someone.

* We are lonely, and sometimes we just need to feel wanted by someone, even for a few moments.

* We have had our self-esteem damaged in the past, and it's easier to hide this online at the start of the, "getting to know you," part of the interaction.

* Sometimes it's easier to see what the other person is looking for before you invest your time and energy getting to know them further.

Online dating is like trying to find the best pair of used underwear at Goodwill, knowing each will have something wrong with them. Everyone deserves to love and to be loved. Just because there are so many people damaged from past relationships doesn't mean that you won't find a person who will match with you. Sometimes you will have common experiences that may help build a bridge to hopefully a healthy relationship. Settling is common for people in these relationships. Shit! I have done this all too often, thinking at the time that it's a better option than being alone - at least we'll have someone, even if they treat us wrong. Sometimes, anything feels better than being alone, for a while, anyway.

So often, I have stayed in toxic relationships just because I thought I didn't deserve anything better. When we feel this way, we tend to stay because we think, or are even made to feel, that we aren't worth love and respect. Wanting more out of a relationship doesn't mean the person you're with is bad. It could just mean that you're just not suitable for one another. I ended up stuck in at least fifty percent of my relationships because, even though I knew, well before it was over, that we shouldn't be together, I stayed. Once the line of disrespect for one another is crossed, it is hard to cross back without remembering what was done or said. You can forgive, but you won't forget what happened in those moments. Each time we forgive and try to move forward, there's a tendency to accept bad behavior more and more often, or to treat someone poorly more and more often, because we no longer even realize we're doing it. It has become second nature.

Many men, in my experience, love the hookup scene; no commitment, never having to see the person again if you don't want to, and your sexual needs and fantasies are fulfilled. Sometimes I don't even know if it is the sexual part or the ego part that needs fulfilling but many people also have a desperate need for feeling wanted. When you have a hookup, it's usually with a random guy who, in essence, "wants" you. So the hookup could be any of these things, just one, or all of them. My outlook has always been that, if it works for them and the other person, great! Just practice safe sex, as your health and the health of others should be your number one priority. There are astronomical amounts of sexual temptation out there, and, no matter how many times I want or crave to just go out and fuck someone who's attractive in my eyes, 99% of the time I stop myself. My mind runs amok, trying to temper my horniness with reason.

Maybe it's my morals, or perhaps it's a lack of self-confidence. Admittedly, the same old reel plays over and over in my head: "I'm not good enough," and I go through the familiar litany of alleged reasons; my weight, my kin, my age, overthinking everything. But sometimes I just crave a particular person in my life - someone to love and hold when things are tough, laugh with during the most random of times, and cry with when life becomes overwhelming and sad. Then my brain (my brain!) comes up with things like: "What if my ideal man comes along, and I have had sex with who-knows-how-many partners? Would this be something he could accept, or would that render a relationship impossible?" Or, "I'm just causing myself to miss out on new and exciting experiences as a gay man, and for what? Someone who may never even show up". Still, I can't help but feel that hookups are something I don't need in my life to be fulfilled as a human being.

Based upon my experiences with and observations of the online dating world, I believe that many people are "Love Virgins." This is a term that I like to use to describe men who have never been told "I love you," by another man, or felt love from a man. This comes into question when a man sleeps around with multiple people in a very short period, and then, "BAM" - just like that, they're in a relationship. The love virgin chases after men and sleeps with whoever is willing, in the hopes that one day a man will say those magic missing words. Chasing dick for love is something that many do. I, myself, am guilty of thinking that sex equals love, yet all I was doing was hoping that I was giving enough of myself to a man for him to "love me," and (of course) to stay. What if, in the midst of all the chasing and all the random hookups, the one who is meant for me, the one who would truly love me, passes by? We would miss our great opportunity, all because we're preoccupied with the notion that hopping on the next dick that comes along might bring love.

It feels and sounds like the mindset of a teenager. You know, the old, "If you don't have sex with him, he will leave you." Fuck! Listen to the voice of experience. Let him leave. Encourage him to leave. He is not worth the headache or the drama that will ensue if it takes sex to keep him happy.

We can't "fuck" our way to happiness without sacrificing a large part of ourselves. Sacrificing or changing ourselves to become someone we're not isn't worth the feeling of fake love, or the continual arguing in the end. If you're giving up your self-respect to rush into something, it isn't the real thing. If it's real, you can't rush it, and you aren't giving up anything. No matter what, your past is your business, and how you view yourself takes top priority. Loving yourself is number one. If you can't do it, no one else is going to be able to. If we let our lives revolve around sex instead of love, will that bring true happiness? Don't get me wrong: sex is great. But can't sex become a poor substitute to fill the void where love should reside in our lives? Or maybe, because we don't know how to deal with our aloneness, we choose random sex for an immediate sense of love.

Looking back on my past relationships, it's crystal clear that I was in them because I was missing true love in my life, and I was staying in hopes that it would one day turn into the love that I longed for. If a relationship doesn't feel right, red flags should start showing themselves in the first month or so of dating, or at the start of a relationship. It's been my experience that red flags mean the guy's not the right fit for you. Relationships have hiccups, but if it has red flags, you need to trust them, and know that red flags now, equals fast-multiplying ones in the future. Trusting someone is the hardest thing to do in this day and age, as people find new, more convincing ways of becoming better players. Some guys make you stop in awe of how gorgeous they are, but that is all it is; the awe of the beauty. Knowing there is trust in my relationship ranks above many other things, including looks, penis size, or finances - it's where it's at for me. Finding trust, and being able to fully trust someone in a relationship, is so rare.

Trust is sexy, and makes me melt. If you find it, I recommend not letting it go over something superficial and minor. All too often, we hide from the truth when we find reality too much to handle, and our heads end up buried in the sand. Paying attention to what is happening around us is the best way to know if what we are doing is best for us. I stop and ask myself all the time, "Why am I looking for a partner in life, instead of just letting things happen?" Past relationships have damaged and hurt me to the point that I sometimes feel I may be allowing my belief in true love to slip away. But love is out there - love so strong that your heart flutters at the very thought of that special person, no matter where you are in the relationship. We all deserve to feel that flutter, and we are all worthy of true love. Giving up isn't an option.

"You don't belong to people forever, so why do we bother trying? Isn't it worth it?" ~ Shelter 2007

The best advice I could give anyone in this life is to have patience, love yourself, and learn to be okay with being alone. Patience is a crucial factor in many things in life. Don't rush it because you want it now; wait on it to naturally happen. We are so used to instant gratification we forget that some of the best things in life take time. As for loving ourselves, many of us may say, "it's easier said than done." If that's true, why do we think we'll find love for another person so quickly, when we can't even love ourselves? We need to be happy with ourselves before we can ever expect happiness with another person. It will be hard to find someone capable of having a higher regard for us than we have for ourselves. Finally, the most significant thing I have learned in this life is accepting and being okay with being alone. If we can't be alone, we will always set ourselves up for relationship failure, as we will always need to have someone with us. We will accept anyone into our lives, just to have that feeling of union and familiarity. Loneliness is one of the hardest things to accept in life. I have learned to be okay with living by myself, but acceptance brings with it days of sadness.

Just when you think you're doing well being alone and independent, you can become overwhelmed with gut-wrenching sadness out of nowhere. Love is a drug that fucks you up in ways you've probably never imagined. The power of love, or even of simple hugs and kisses from another person is unbelievably comforting; again, reasons why people will take a hookup or any interaction that comes along. We need to do what makes us happy, as long as we will also be pleased with our decisions after the fact as well. You do you!

I'm not the only person, when asked, "How are you?" lies and replies, "I am doing fine!" while inside, our hearts are breaking, and we feel like we're dying inside. It's all hard to go through, and harder to accept, but we will make it - even on our darkest days.

TRUTHS BE TOLD

....

CHAPTER 9

"We're all perfectly imperfect."

ruth be told, I hope there is a time in my life that my days don't seem so filled with darkness and sorrow, and I can feel like I am allowed to live instead of always having to be solely responsible because others are not. Darkness looms over me, and I can't help feeling that I am expected just to do what is needed or required of me and not be happy. The truth is, I feel like my happiness has never mattered to anyone in this world. I don't even think my happiness has mattered to me, and now that I am looking for it, it seems like the world is angry with me. Thinking about my joy and looking at what I want out of life through my experiences has helped me. Like many things in my life, this too has helped mould me into the man that I am today. Without all of the darkness in my life, who knows where I would be. Some people have come across my path in life that have expressed that they believe that I am far from a man because of how I came out and how I live my life.

Okay! Everyone can have their opinions, secrets, lies, misery and cast their judgements on people. However, if that is what it truly takes for them to be 100% happy with themselves, so be it, just don't go causing others misery because you have nowhere else to place yours. We are all perfectly imperfect and have had things happen in our lives that make us ...well, us! My thoughts and truths may come off to people as judgemental, wrong, inconsiderate or selfish, well this is who I am and how I see life through my eyes from everything that I have lived through or witnessed. Some of my truths are more about all the regrets I have in life. Over time I have made small notes of my thoughts and truths in no specific order.

My truths about my children

* The truth is, I hope my children know how much I loved them to stay and be there for them. I'm sure to some point they resent me for what I did to our family.
* The truth is the love I hold for my children is genuine and unconditional. I'm sure it hasn't always seemed that way for them. There were times I was present yet absent, all simultaneously well trying to figure out myself. For that, I will always be genuinely and deeply sorry.

✽ The truth is, I would rather my children and I be upset with each other for some time because we spoke our truth. To me, this is better than us holding in the truth and allowing the guilt caused by it to eat away at one of us. The last thing I would ever want is my kids to suffer because of something I did that they can't come and talk to me about.

✽ The truth is, I'm at the point in my life as a parent that I have begun to fear the future. I don't know if it's because my kids are the age of moving forward with their lives away from home or if it's my fear of being alone. I hope my children find their true happiness and that they're never lonely in this world.

My truths and thoughts about men

✽ The truth is most men seem to think that their penises make them a man. It takes more than an appendage to make you a man.

✽ The truth is, most men send their pictures of their body and dick; the problem with these kinds of selfies is you can't see a person's true character in those photos. These kinds of pictures show nothing but big dick energy, and it's not a turn-on. It's more of a turn-off to the extent of making a guy who was erect and turning him as erect as an elastic band, just as I am sure it dries up a woman like the Sahara Desert.

* The truth is most of the pictures of your cock that you think are great aren't. A good percentage of the people that receive them from you just treat it like the macaroni art a child brings home. Oh, that's beautiful! Did you make it yourself? I love how you used all that glitter! Did you have help with it? Yet, in my head, I am thinking, he shouldn't have taken it at that angle! What made him think that was a good picture? WTF! Does he know what it looks like? Is it supposed to look like that? Why? Just why?

* The truth is sex should be about finding new and exciting ways of climaxing during sex, but this doesn't mean you can't do it with the same person for decades without cheating or having an open relationship.

* The truth is, I believe most times when men hookup with someone, it's because it helps with one of four things unless they're a Love Virgin

  1. To mask the feelings of rejection from the last person they were with.
  2. To cope with the feelings of lonesomeness.
  3. To boost one's ego.
  4. Excitement.

My truths and thoughts on life

✱ The truth is to make peace with the past even when it seems impossible to do. When you're always looking back, it's hard to see what is in front of you.

✱ The truth is one of the hardest life lessons is having to learn to take care of your responsibilities. This includes financial responsibilities, paying what you owe before anything and stop worrying about having extra money so that you can buy things you don't even need. One of the best feelings is truly knowing you don't owe anything to anyone.

✱ The truth is life is short, and we never know when it will end. Live your life knowing you're happy today, with the knowledge that your decisions today can become a new reality tomorrow or even tomorrow's guilt. So, if you're going to do something on a whim, take a second beforehand and think of how it will affect you tomorrow.

Truth…

✱ The truth is, I have witnessed how short life is.

✱ The truth is, I have seen a child lose their life at a young age and what it can do to the family.

✱ The truth is, I have seen and heard a man trapped inside a car after a car wreck, hearing this young man in his early twenties burn to death. I listened to his last words gurgle from him, his cries for help and his final goodbyes before the fire took his life will never be forgotten.

* The truth is, I have witnessed many family members and friends die of several things, including Alzheimer's disease, cancer, lung disease and more.
* The truth is, no matter what age you're, make the most out of each day that you're here on this earth.
* The truth is, I wish I had known. I wish I had the chance to say goodbye.

My truths

* The truth is, I wake up from dreams, wishing you were here and you're not. I wonder how I could have changed that.
* The truth is people say that Connie raped me in the first few years of our relationship as I was not of consensual age for sex in Canada. Maybe in the eye of the law, but I don't feel that I was. I knew what I was doing even though I was not sixteen when we started having sex.
* The truth is, I would never have stayed with Connie even if I wasn't gay.
* The truth is, I feel like I drowned in my marriage. How could Connie watch me work so hard to try and keep the family afloat while doing so little to help? This, to me, was just a selfish move on her part. Our relationship was 80/20 at best, and this caused me to have feelings

of sadness. The most important thing I believe is that Connie took a part of my youth from me by the things she didn't contribute to our marriage and family. Even though I was a father and knew what I was doing, I felt that I could have had parts of my youth. Being a teenager and so maxed out with responsibilities caused me grave stress from just trying to survive. Had there been equal responsibility between Connie and me, perhaps I may have been able to do more age-appropriate things occasionally. However, this never happened. Ever!

✱ The truth is if you want to survive and have a long-lasting relationship, treat each day like you're still trying to win that person over. Always bring them flowers, just because. Don't let the butterflies stop fluttering.

From everything that I have witnessed and my experiences, one of the most significant truths is that two men cannot love without rules and limitations. Many of these rules and restrictions are put in place by one person, if not both in the relationship and not so much from society as we would think. It almost seems as time goes on, most relationships will be open relationships, and monogamy will practically be a thing of the past. Is sleeping with multiple men when in a relationship love?

FINDING DANTE

....

CHAPTER 10

"Every piece of the puzzle that doesn't fit
gets you closer to the answer."
~Cynthia Lewis

My life has been a slow journey, filled with many moments of love, happiness, pain and sadness. My choices and actions have dictated the paths taken, whether good or bad. Through the years, I have grown and matured into the man I am now, and with each passing day I strive to find peace in every moment. Though some of the paths I chose failed to lead me in the direction of emotional or mental stability, they all combined to mold me into who I am. All of my paths are essentially pieces of the crazy puzzle that is my life.

Dante, my faithful Dante, is out there in the world somewhere, and I know that he will come along when I'm least expecting it. My Dante may not be what I have imagined in my mind, but if he is a man who has respect, love, trust and honesty for me - well, that's better than looks or sex any day in my book. Ideally, my Dante will be old enough to remember significant events that have occurred in my lifetime, rather than only knowing about them from history class or online memes. Events such as the deaths of Princess Diana, Michael Jackson, and Mother Teresa; 9/11 and President George W. Bush's declaration of war. I need someone who remembers using a landline phone, and stretching the receiver cord until you hear your parent(s) yelling at you to stop stretching the cord, or it's going to end up staying that way. Someone who remembers when privacy on the phone meant being crouched down in a corner of the nearest closet. Someone who knows what it was like growing up without the technology of the internet, and if we wanted to masturbate, we had to use images from a magazine or movie poster in our room. Someone whose pornhub.com was seeing the bulge on a baseball player in his pro-flare pants, or naked pictures in National Geographic Magazine.

In my youth, there was no instant access to hardcore porn as there is today. We had to use our imaginations, let the anticipation build, and wait for our alone time to do the deed. One would think that men like myself, who grew up before the 1990s, would be much better at foreplay than those who have always relied on instant porn. If my Dante doesn't know the struggle of finding a specific moment in a movie on a VHS tape, there is a good chance he is too young for me. If he only knows the convenience of a cell phone, and doesn't remember the annoyance (yet also pure awesomeness) of having a pager, he's probably too young for me. Having once owned a Nokia cell phone, then experiencing the thrill of getting the all-new Motorola Razor flip phone, and having to use the number keypad to "type" out text messages, may make you old enough to ride this ride.

After years of searching, and trying to make relationships work with people who have had many different experiences, and who have vastly different outlooks on life, I finally realize what I need to make me happy. Dante and I must be able to communicate intimately and honestly, without the need for electronic devices: no memes or text messages will be required to show our love for one another. For me, this would be hitting the jackpot. But, before I can expect to find these qualities in someone else, I must first find them within myself. Then I can be assured Dante is searching for me as ardently as I search for him. Our accomplishments, adventures, and simple joys are always better when we have someone we love to share them with. One day I will have that special someone to bear witness to my life.

Back in 2003, I had a co-worker who was more than forty years my senior. One day, she stopped me as I was working and asked me if I could come with her for a minute. She took me to the dining area, where we had a clear view of customers sitting at the tables. She motioned to a couple sitting at a table for two. "You see those two people sitting there?". I replied, "Yes, what about them?" She looked straight into my eyes: "don't ever let that happen to you," she said. They were sitting there; approximately mid-to-late seventies, if not older. They were sitting, coffee in front of them, the wife blankly staring out the window as the cars passed by. Her husband sat with the newspaper in front of his face, and neither spoke a word to one another. My co-worker was a very wise and extraordinary woman. She also advised me not to wait for special occasions to buy a loved one flowers. Her final piece of wisdom: never forget to tell your partner that you love them, even when you are seventy-plus and sitting silently at a table for two. Let them know how much they mean to you.

As my co-worker spoke these words, I could see the pain in her eyes, and knew that her words were coming from experience. I was about twenty years old when she told me these things, and I treasure the wisdom that she was kind enough to share that day. Don't become so complacent in your relationship that you grow numb to the spark that initially started your relationship in the first place. Why put something as small as a newspaper, between you and someone who is (or should be) your whole life? Don't chance stupidity in your relationship. If you're fortunate enough to find the love of your life, why risk it? They might not be there for the rest of your life!

There are times when we feel so broken, we just aren't able to pick up the pieces of our lives alone. If you're lucky enough to have or find a partner who is there for you, hold on to that person if they're willing to stick around when things fall apart. People come into our lives for a reason, and though that reason may be unclear, one day we will understand why. Just don't let the why come too late! Lead the way and set the tone, be there when the world seems to be dark and dreary for your partner. Sometimes all it takes is simply holding them, letting them know you're there, and assuring them that it will be okay. The power of a hug and the words "It's going to be okay! I love you!" is extraordinary.

When we feel the weight of the world on our shoulders, knowing that we're loved and cared for has the power to let us reset and refocus. The times that I have been there for my partner, but they weren't able to give the same support to me, are countless. At times, the world has left me feeling so defeated and broken, and all I needed was the touch of another person, comforting me and telling me that I would be okay. As silly as it may sound, it indeed can be the best medicine for a broken soul. One of the cruelest things that can happen in a relationship is giving all you have to the person you love, but when you're the one suffering, you are left to deal with it alone. Your suffering becomes more complex, and you have new anxieties that stem from wondering what you did wrong, or what you didn't do, to make the one you love desert you in your time of need. I have suffered in silence most of my life, never having had the support I needed from my partner at the time. Often I would wake up in the middle of the night, practically in tears, curled up to their back as they slept, because that was the closest thing to a human touch I could get, unless of course, it was the touch indicating they wanted sex. There is no amount of sex that can help you genuinely feel comfort and love from another, no matter how many times they grunt "I love you!" as they are about to climax.

After more than a decade of experience with men, and having been engaged three times during that time, I have learned a few things. In a relationship, some people come off as not caring enough to show you the love and support you need, but the truth is, often they just don't know how to show it. Some men never learned how to support another person, but establishing the fundamentals of mutual communication at the start of a relationship should go far towards promoting reciprocal demonstrations of love and support. If someone truly cares for you, they will find ways of letting you know. But, if they don't put forth any effort, it may be time to walk away. Again, this comes from my experiences, so when your partner doesn't appear to support you, trust me, it's because he doesn't want to.

One man I dated, but to whom I was never engaged, showed me more love and support than all of my fiancés combined, but it ended when we both realized we were in different places in our lives. This experience, however, was a genuine eye-opener. It showed me how, for years, I had been settling in my relationships with men, out of loneliness. This wasn't easy to accept about myself. I had been saying, "yes," to men who proposed marriage, who couldn't even show me basic love and support. Even after this hard realization, I still found it difficult to end a relationship when I could see it wasn't working. Continuing with a relationship was a way of not being lonely, even when I knew it was toxic, not only for me, but also for my partner. Once you start to become miserable in a relationship, you typically end up saying or doing things that you know you shouldn't. I personally have done things AND said things while in relationships that I regret. There are no acceptable excuses, even though it felt, at the time, like I was hanging on the edge of a cliff, and the only way to avoid plummeting to my death was to spew hurtful words, no matter how true. When we are hurting on the inside, we tend to become someone that we normally would despise; someone unrecognizable.

Each of these experiences pointed me towards what I truly need to be happy, loved, and supported. Dante is a fictional character, born from years of suppressing who I was, and he's at least partially responsible for my unrealistic expectations when it comes to men. Dante, however, also gave me a reason to not give up on the hope that someone exists, somewhere in this world, just for me. Just because someone doesn't fit in my life at the moment, it doesn't mean it couldn't work out in the future. Everything I have done in my life has been a stepping stone to the next big thing. Without those steps, it's a challenging walk uphill. At times we may trip on the way up, but as long as we get back up, we travel on, stronger and wiser. I have tripped and fallen face-first over people I thought could be my Dante, and it sometimes took me years to clear my head and get back on my feet when I discovered they weren't.

If I were to look back on my life, even five years ago, I would probably laugh at myself for the things that I allowed to happen. Why did I paint the red flags green? Why? Dammit, because I needed to stop feeling so fucking alone in the world - that's why. I tried to create my own Dante out of broken men; men who needed help fixing themselves before they could ever enter into a healthy relationship. Not only were these men broken: I was as well. Pairing two broken people is like dropping and shattering two glasses on the ground, then trying to glue the pieces back together - it's impossible. It has been better for me to stay single and fix myself, emotionally and mentally, before trying to be there for anyone else. It's me first, because, if I don't have me, no one else does either. So, the chase for Dante has ended. My years of waiting, hoping, and trying to create this fantasy character has been a fucking waste of time, and I only recently discovered why.

Dating and love are real - it's not meant to be reality television with a scripted cast. You genuinely do get back what you put forth into the world, so if you're broken, you will attract the broken. Face it: if broken is our standard, we can't see what whole and healthy looks like. When we are healthy, and we have fixed in our head what we need for our own mental health, we can see more clearly, and we can spot someone else who is in a reasonably healthy frame of mind. The red flags no longer need to be painted green because it is easier to see healthy versus unhealthy. People may claim that I am, "too picky," or ,"too specific," in what I am looking for in a partner, and I must say, I disagree. After years of self-discovery, I know what it takes to make me happy. I also know what I cannot accept in a relationship.

Waiting on someone to work on themselves only slows our growth and progress, because we naturally want to help others. Getting involved with another person includes becoming part of whatever drama they're dealing with too, and just isn't healthy. I have found that, if I stay away from unnecessary drama, I can focus more on my own well-being. In a world of technology and social media, we have fresh drama thrust in our faces every time we open an app on our phones. That drama can eventually seem normal, if you let it in. Normalizing drama harms us, whether in our own self or within a relationship. We see people on social media and in real life, constantly over-sharing their issues, until it becomes accepted as normal, and we begin to believe that unhappiness should be, not only expected, but shared. Social media is nothing but smoke and mirrors: it's all an illusion, and we have come to accept everything as we see it, without further investigation. Oh, the times I have met someone face to face after speaking online, and they weren't at all like the persona they created on social media, or on an app. It has to be at least 90% of them! We all create our Dante on social media. We create what we want or even need, to try and make ourselves feel whole.

Be the person you want to find!

That line, right there, is the reason my search for Dante has come to an end. Dante is all of the things that I have wanted in a guy. He is what I have been giving and offering every man I have, dated, had sex with, or been engaged to. The standards I set for myself were below par, but I continued to give and give. Just like the saying goes, "I wear my heart on my sleeve." I allowed myself to be walked on and used to the extent that, in desperation, I conjured up a magical person who was waiting out there, just for me. That just is not the case. There is no magic. But, the right person IS out there for me, and we will blend and mesh perfectly. All the qualities that Dante in my mind possessed, are the same ones I had been offering the men I was involved with. I am Dante!

THROUGH THE DARKNESS

....

CHAPTER 11

***"People don't build walls to keep people out,
they build walls to see who will break
them down"***

Sometimes, finding your light means you have to pass through the darkness. Do I wish I could say I feel happy all the time? Of course, I do! Whenever I wake up, I wish I could say that I feel joy and love, yet I still have days when I feel nothing but sadness over some of the things that I have allowed to happen to me. Feeling incomplete, like something is missing, still hits me hard out of nowhere, almost like a clown jumping out of a closet in a horror movie. BAM! There it is, a massive gut-wrenching feeling that I am not enough, and THAT must be why I am alone.

Maybe if I change who I am, change my morals, my beliefs, and forget about the value I put on myself, then perhaps I will find the one for me, and no longer feel alone.

Maybe…because most likely, if I did those things, I would feel guilt and shame for allowing myself to go against everything I believe in, to conform to today's new norms, and that is not me. So, I will continue to do things that bring me moments and memories of happiness, and I will continue to grasp onto them like they're my last breath of air. Do I know why I feel like this? Most of the time, no! Do I understand that the feeling will pass? Yes, of course, it will! Each new beginning starts in the dark, just as a new seed, deep in the ground, is only days or weeks away from seeing the light. If we want to find our way to the light, we must nurture ourselves for positive growth. We must ensure lots of self-love, self-care, and room to plant our new roots in the soil. New beginnings are presented to us all the time, and it depends on how blinded we are by everything happening in our lives, whether or not we take a chance.

We may not know where it will take us, which can (and will) cause anxiety. I don't know where my next journey will lead me, or how that journey will end, but whenever I get that all-too familiar feeling of falling or struggling, I have to remind myself to get back up. Each time we fall and get back up, it makes us stronger, wiser, and prevents, or at least softens, similar falls in the future. Let the process of change happen, give yourself room to grow, and see where change takes you. Falling autumn leaves signal change. Similarly, anxiety, sadness, and tears accompany endings and beginnings in life. Remember, without that falling of the leaves, there will be no winter. Without winter, we have no spring. If we don't allow ourselves the time to be sad and regretful, to recover, and to relearn how to love ourselves, there will be no growth, no warmth, no brighter days ahead.

There were times in my life when I didn't have to stay, feeling stuck and dormant. Walking away was always an option, just as it is for anyone. The number of times I thought about what it would be like if I just walked away would be impossible to count. But, each time such ideas entered my mind, my thoughts would shift to the love I have for my kids. I know my children harbor some resentment towards me, probably more than what most kids hold towards a parent. I know that they have hated me, at points in their lives. We clashed at times, and sometimes we still do. I tried my best. I know it may have been hard for them to always see it, but I did try. Just as I'm sure I have done things that caused pain and left emotional scars which, of course, were unintentional, I too have emotional scars from my life. If only I could heal their scars; change things that happened, and make it better, I would do it all in a split second.

All of these years, I feel like I've been standing on an emotional cliff, just waiting on a push, or for the courage to jump. Thoughts of failure and feelings of pain rush through me all the time. What if I hadn't made the choices that I made? Would my kids have had to go through as much suffering as they did? Would they have had a more uncomplicated childhood had I stayed in the closet, and with Connie? These are things that I know I will never have the answers to, but I can't stop myself from wondering, what if? I feel like the weight of the world is on my shoulders, and I hold it there, almost like a punishment for being who I am. When I don't help someone, but I have the power to do so, I feel unbearably guilty, even when I know that the person in need could, and should, be learning to help themself. No one can go through life with someone always holding their hand. This comes off harsh to some, but we're not handed a parenting handbook when our kids are born. Even if we were, most of us would use it about as often as the Bible, and, just like the Bible, that handbook would be open to interpretation.

Was coming out selfish of me? I guess in some ways, it was. But, everyone deserves their own shot at happiness, and just because some of our decisions may not benefit everyone around us, it doesn't mean that past choices must haunt us forever. If someone has kids and is in an emotionally abusive relationship, most would say it's a no-brainer: leave. If someone has to hide who they are, it's a form of emotional abuse and change has to take place, to promote emotional healing and self-esteem. We can only protect our children from so much in life, and we want our kids to be as happy as possible. That's what I wanted for my kids while Connie and I were ending our relationship. At some point, I hope they understood that I could have walked away and didn't. They meant more to me than anything else, and I stayed for them. I don't want recognition or a medal; I just want them to know that, no matter how hard it got, I always chose them. In many ways, I feel like my guilt has kept me from being a great parent. Sometimes, instead of being stern, with them, I was too relaxed, fearing I could lose their love. I've never been willing to risk that for the possibility of personal happiness. Life lesson: Don't stop being you out of fear. You've made it this far in life; being who you are won't change the past, but it will determine the future. Be you!

Love. I just want to feel love the same way I give it. When I feel it, I want to hold his hand until the end of our time here on earth together. When we are old, if one of us is in a wheelchair, the other one will push him in his wheelchair down to the beach at sunset. I want to love until there is nothing left to give. I want the little things, like stopping together to look at the leaves changing color, and listening to the breeze as it releases them, allowing them to fall from the trees in the autumn. I want someone with whom I can drive, and have the sunroof open with music blasting, singing the worst karaoke you could imagine. I want to live, and I want to take chances. When I find my suitor, I will give him my trust, but it is up to him what he does with it.

What can I say? I was lost, but now I am found. The only one who needed to be okay with me was me. I sat, ashamed of myself many nights of my life, caught up in my thoughts and overthinking, crying, worrying that everything I did was a horrible mistake. The only true error I made, and we all tend to make this one at some point, was doubting myself, causing me to try and cover up my insecurities.

What do I hope you take from all of this? Be the person you want to find in life, and don't ever let others hold you back from living life to the fullest. No one is changing the way they live because of you. They're still living their best life, so why shouldn't you? Life is a wild ride: ride it, and let the waves take you to the place that you deserve to be. There will be dark days, but once the sky has cleared, you will see that it was all worth it in the end. Would I change the way things played out now, looking back on my life? Never! Not once! I found my way through the hardest of days, which molded me into the person I am today. Never give up on yourself! I found my way through the darkness, and so will you. WE ARE ENOUGH!

Love,
James

STARTING THE NEXT CHAPTER

"FATE"

*"A person often meets his destiny
on the road he took to avoid it."*
~ Jean de La Fontaine

S ince the original release of I AM ENOUGH, in October 2021, many things have changed. A short time before the release, I met someone wonderful. My mind told me to keep him at bay, and not move forward, but my heart said otherwise. Thankfully, this man was persistent, even when I explained the reasons for my hesitation. He told me to believe, and let fate do its magic. So I decided not to listen to the past, which always seems to echo in my head.

What can I say? He was right, and now I am happy that I took that leap, and allowed, as he would say, "fate," to run its course. If I have learned anything over the years, it's that one's life experiences, no matter their age, truly determine who they are. My charming and handsome better-half may not remember the Princess Diana tragedy, or some other historical events, as I had hoped. But, he has touched me in so many ways that I am truly grateful for. His love has shown me that it's okay to trust again. The love and compassion he exudes is remarkable. When I look into his hazel eyes, I see home: I see my future.

Don't give up on the hope that love exists for everyone. I closed the last chapter, and before I knew it, my prince was there, waiting. Our families are now blended, with six children in total, ranging from 3 years old to 24. I can only imagine what the coming decades will hold (grandchildren, perhaps?). He and I are set to be married in the fall of 2023. Currently, we reside in Ontario, Canada, living life to its fullest.

Trust your heart. You never know where it may lead, or, who it may lead you to.

SAVING THE BEST
FOR LAST

• •

ACKNOWLEDGMENTS

My thank you's, can't be expressed enough in this acknowledgement to the amazing person who co-edited this edition of the book with me. S.J. Cuthbertson, your hard work and dedication to this book over the last numerous months, holds a special place with me. Your time, frustration, and skills have not gone unrecognized. The kindness you have shown is remarkable, and shines above it all, and many could take away important life lessons from you. Thank you from the bottom of my heart for helping to make one's dream even better. Most of all, thank you for being my friend.

Printed in Great Britain
by Amazon

39701830R00108